The Colonial Dollhouse

How to Make Your Own Early American Dollhouse with Colonial Furniture and Accessories for under $50.

Phyllis Gift Jellison

VNR VAN NOSTRAND REINHOLD COMPANY
New York Cincinnati Toronto London Melbourne

Photographs by Ron Bergeson, photographer for the University of New Hampshire, Durham, New Hampshire.

Dolls and bird nesting in the eaves are of bisque using old molds by Christine Packard of Willimantic, Maine

Copyright (c) 1977 by Litton Educational Publishing, Inc.
Library of Congress Catalog Card Number 76-42594
ISBN 0-442-24129-1

Printed in the United States of America
Designed by Loudan Enterprise

Published in 1977 by Van Nostrand Reinhold Company
A division of Litton Educational Publishing, Inc.
450 West 33rd Street, New York, NY 10001, U.S.A.

Van Nostrand Reinhold Limited
1410 Birchmount Road, Scarborough, Ontario M1P 2E7, Canada

Van Nostrand Reinhold Australia Pty. Limited
17 Queen Street, Mitcham, Victoria 3132, Australia

Van Nostrand Reinhold Company Limited
Molly Millars Lane, Wokingham, Berkshire, England

16 15 14 13 12 11 10 9 8 7 6 5 4 3 2 1

Library of Congress Cataloging in Publication Data

Jellison, Phyllis Gift.
    The colonial dollhouse.

    Includes index.
    1. Doll-houses.   2. United States—Social life and customs—Colonial period, ca. 1600–1775.   I. Title.
TT175.3.J44   745.59′23   76-42594
ISBN 0-442-24129-1

Contents

PREFACE 5

INTRODUCTION 5

THE DOLLHOUSE 6
TOOLS 6
SUPPLIES 6
DIRECTIONS 7

FURNITURE CONSTRUCTION 54
TOOLS 54
BASIC TECHNIQUES 55

FURNITURE PATTERNS AND DIRECTIONS 58
KEEPING ROOM 58
PARLOR 66
BACK HALL 76
BLUE BEDROOM 77
RED BEDROOM 85
BATH 92
WEAVING ROOM 95
HIRED GIRL'S ROOM 101

ACCESSORIES 105
TINWARE 107
WOOD ACCESSORIES 111
CARDBOARD ACCESSORIES 120
CLAY ACCESSORIES 122
FABRIC ACCESSORIES 122
 LOOR COVERINGS 122
BOOK DIRECTIONS 125

INDEX 127

Preface

I started on my mini-adventures with the Colonial Doll-house. I had no previous experience in the art of making miniature dollhouses, or dollhouse furniture, though I was eager to learn. This enthusiasm plus some invaluable help from my good friend and neighbor, Mary Hinckley, a doll-house devotee, enabled me to work on the Dollhouse with confidence and genuine enjoyment. I hope that this book will provide you with the same stimulation and guidance I received from all those who shared their know-how with me.

Ideally, a miniaturist, like any craftsman, should have a work area that can be left undisturbed, where tools and supplies can be spread out and easily accessible. Unfortunately, this is not always possible. I managed (as will some of you) to make do by working out of a supply box, sometimes in my husband's study, but more often on the family-room table where I could supervise the family, answer the phone, and hover over dinner at the same time.

The Colonial Dollhouse and furniture cost me about twenty-five dollars to construct. It certainly will not cost you more than fifty dollars. I used, for the most part, inexpensive materials, and odds and ends of supplies on hand—scraps of mat board left over from picture framing, fabric remnants, and a variety of leftover paints and wood finishes. I also had access to my son's basic woodworking tools and his lumber supply for the posts and beams used in the construction of the house.

Incidentally, I should mention that I had the advantage of a certain amount of free labor: my twenty-year-old daughter, Jody, made the Pennsylvania Dutch dry sink, patterned after one in our own home; my fourteen-year-old son, Tom, made the writing bench in the hired girl's room; while twelve-year-old Sally served as overall supervisor and critic and helped clothe the dolls. My husband, Charles, edited the manuscript with unflagging good humor and hardly a grimace over my uncontrollable urge to ramble.

As to the quality of your first efforts, don't worry if your craftsmanship is less than perfect. Above all, don't be discouraged if you experience a few failures in making tiny items. Results improve with a little practice or a new approach. Remember, many of today's antique pieces were homemade by "country folk" and were quaintly imperfect.

My efforts were rewarding and opened the door to a fascinating new world—the world of miniatures.

Introduction

The Colonial Dollhouse was born one rainy Saturday afternoon when my daughter Sally brought home a large cardboard carton and announced that she was going to build a dollhouse. She also brought home four or five smaller cartons that she intended to use inside the large one for individual rooms. Of course, they weren't the right size, and so she called on me for help. From that point on, I became so involved with the project that I neglected my family shamefully until, three months later, the house was completely furnished and ready to move into, right down to the bird's nest in the eaves and the sliced bread on the kitchen table.

The problem of creating individual rooms was overcome when I decided to create a second story by cutting up another large carton for floors, and supporting them atop rectangular pieces of wood in each corner of the box. Voila—corner posts! Having commited my house to Early-American corner posts (seldom used after 1800), I decided that my dollhouse (Notice how it has ceased to be my daughter's dollhouse.) should be representative of the Revolutionary War period, in keeping with our nation's Bicentennial celebration. This decision gave me direction and a theme.

I researched the period so that a way of life would be authentically reproduced. A family took form in my imagination: The wife would be from Pennsylvania, (my birthplace), and she would meet and marry a young New Englander (as I did) who was engaged in commerce in Portsmouth, New Hampshire. By late spring of 1776 the couple would have their own home and two children, a boy of four and a baby daughter.

The house is a typical two-story New England town house, painted barn red with white trim. It could have been built in the old Maritime quarter once known as Puddle Dock, and part of the original site of Portsmouth, which was first called Strawbery (sic) Banke. The windows are the newer English style, following leaded casements, of double-hung wooden sashes and small panes of blown glass. Clapboards were used for wall coverings in New England and shingles for the high pitch roofs (owing to the heavy snow and "Noreasters" common to the region). No doubt there would have been out-buildings as well in which to store food and other supplies, but that's another project.

The furniture is authentic for the period and I have given a brief description of some of the more interesting pieces as an introduction to the various rooms.

The Dollhouse

The Colonial Dollhouse started as a rectangular cardboard carton. The dimensions are scaled one inch to the foot, and aside from the unusually high ceilings (9″ instead of the more traditional 7″ or 8″), this scale worked out well for my carton. After the beams and floors were in place, the ceilings looked lower anyway, so I was glad that I had proceeded with the carton I had. A different size carton and room arrangement could be substituted but you will then have to work out different dimensions. The house can also be made from plywood as long as the inside dimensions remain the same.

In building your dollhouse and dollhouse furniture, you may wish to substitute other materials for the ones specified here. What materials you choose will depend on what you have on hand, which materials you are comfortable working with, etc. In many cases mat board and balsa wood can be used interchangeably.

Mat board is a sturdy cardboard that can be purchased at most art shops. I used it for the roof shingles, bases for the fireplaces and chimneys, and for most of the trim and molding on the inside and outside of the house. However, another similar weight cardboard can be substituted (1/16″ thick) or balsa wood may be preferred. (Familiarize yourself with the properties of balsa wood by reading the furniture section on Tools and Basic Construction Techniques.) Mat board does not take a stain as satisfactorily as wood and you may want to stain, rather than paint the trim, as I have. Balsa wood is just as strong as mat board and it has the advantage of being easier to cut. Also, it can be purchased in the correct width needed for the trim which eliminates a lot of cutting. The one big disadvantage of balsa wood is that it is considerably more expensive.

The tools you will need depend to some extent on what materials you are working with. For instance, balsa wood can be cut with the same knife you will use for the furniture. Mat board, on the other hand, requires a heavy duty knife. The following lists of tools and supplies are all you will need to build the dollhouse with the directions and patterns given.

TOOLS

Knife: If working with mat board, use a Stanley utility knife or X-acto knife handle #5 or #6 with #25 blades. If working with balsa wood or cardboard, use X-acto knife handle #1 or #2 with #11 blades.
Miter box or plastic angles
Saw
Staple gun
Scissors
Metal-edged ruler with cork back (for cutting balsa)
Yardstick
Hammer
Nail punch (small point for 1″ finishing nails)
Wood block for sanding
Cutting board
Brushes, pencils, tweezers, and metal weight (for back-up when toenailing or stapling)

SUPPLIES

1 rectangular cardboard carton 24″ long, 18″ high, 16 1/2″ deep, and 1/8″ thick, with no top and a single bottom piece (a common size)
3 large cardboard cartons at least 24″ × 18″ and 1/8″ thick
1 piece of plywood 24 1/2″ × 24 1/2″ × 3/4″
25 1″ finishing nails
10 large-head roofing nails (short lengths)
4 yards pine-pattern contact paper for floors
8″ white contact paper for window dividers
1 permanent-ink, black, felt-tip pen with medium size round point
White mending tape such as Mystik or Scotch plastic tape
1 piece white mat board for fireplaces and chimneys
1 piece white mat board 1/16″ thick (if used for trim)
2 pieces gray mat board (if used for roof shingles)
1 quart white gesso (Hyplar's, Liquitex)
1 quart white modeling paste (if you decide to make your own bricks)
1 small tube black acrylic paint (for coloring the modeling paste)
1 piece lightweight tin 18 7/8″ × 3″ (for the steps)
Pine wood stain (Min-wax or your favorite stain)
Varnish (mat or dull finish)
White glue
Epoxy clear-drying glue
Sand paper, both fine and medium
Acrylic house paint of your color choice
4 packages "Sculpey" (for bricks) or dollhouse "brick" paper
1/3 yard wallpaper or fabric for each bedroom (2/3 yards for both)
1 yard clear medium-weight plastic for windows (40″ wide)
Straight pins; crayon pine-wood stick; miniature straw flowers; "train-yard" grass or sandpaper; scraps of cheesecloth, fine cotton fabric or typing paper (for hinges)

BALSA WOOD

15 pieces 36″ × 3/8″ × 1/16″ (if used for trim)
1 piece 36″ × 1/4″ × 1/16″ (if used for trim)
10 pieces 36″ × 4″ × 1/16″ (if used for roof and outside trim)
1 piece 36″ × 3″ × 1/8″ (for Dutch door and shelves)
7 pieces 36″ × 1/8″ × 1/32″ (to cover exposed edges)
2 pieces 36″ × 3″ × 1/16″ (for inside doors)

PINE WOOD

1 piece 26 1/2″ × 1 1/8″ × 3/8″ (for ridge beam)

25' × 3/4" square (for posts and beams)
8' × 3/8" × 3/4" (for roof)
6' × 1/2" × 1/4" (for roof)
4 1/2" of 3/8" dowel (for stair post)
16" of 1/8" dowel (for ladder)

DIRECTIONS

1. Mount the carton on a piece of plywood 24 1/4" × 24 1/4" × 3/4" thick. I purposely positioned the carton to the rear of the plywood to allow the extra width of plywood (7 3/4") in front of the house for an outdoor garden. (Actually, the garden side of the house is the rear entrance, but since it provides access to the working area, I have referred to it as the front.) I used Elmer's glue throughout the project, but any white glue will work well. After gluing the carton in place, nail its bottom to the plywood with short, large-headed roofing nails for reinforcement.

2. For easy access to the interior, the front (or garden) side of the carton is cut away. (You may wish to do this before the carton is positioned on the plywood.) This cut-out piece can be used for the upstairs floor, but you will need additional cardboard for the attic floor, wall partitions, and the roof structure. (Eventually, all exposed cardboard edges will be covered with balsa wood strips the exact width of the edge and glued into place.)

3. Cut two pieces of cardboard 24" × 16 1/2" for the upstairs and attic floors. Cut a 7 1/2" × 3" hole in one of the pieces to provide for the steps to the upstairs. (Fig. 1) Cut a 3" × 3" hole in the other piece for ladder access to the attic. (Fig. 2)

4. Cover all three floors with pine-pattern contact paper. With a permanent-ink felt-tip pen, line the contact paper to look like random-width floor boards with pegs. The floors should fit rather tightly into the carton, without bending. If the floors (and partitions) do not fit perfectly, mending tape can be used later to cover the cracks. Baseboards will also cover cracks around the edges, when they are added later on. Fit but do not secure the floors.

5. The upright corner posts (14 altogether) are 8 7/8" × 3/4" × 3/4" pine. Cut and stain (or paint, if you prefer) seven of the posts on all sides for the first floor. Glue one post into each of the four corners inside the carton. Toenail at the base, using 1" finishing nails, and set with a nail punch. Hold a heavy metal weight behind post while driving the nails in place. Fill holes with a pine-colored crayon stick. Reinforce posts by stapling (with a gun) outside the carton, using a metal backup as before. (Fig. 3) (The front posts could be made 8 1/8" high instead of 8 7/8" high so that the ceiling beam can rest directly on top of the posts and extend all the way across the front of the house. The two rear beams in the keeping room and the "blue" bedroom, which is above the keeping room—the other bedroom is "red"—could also be cut shorter. This beam-on-post construction would be authentic and more stable.)

6. Toenail two more posts at the center front, each 9" from the outside walls and 3" from each other for the doorway. (See Fig. 12) Place one more post at the rear in the center section 9" from the outside wall but do not nail or staple it in. This post will later become the right corner post in the keeping room.

7. The room partitions should be worked on outside the house. The partition that separates the kitchen from the parlor is made from a piece of cardboard 15 3/4" × 8 7/8", in which two holes are cut for doors, each 6 1/2" high and 2 5/16" wide. (Fig. 4)

8. The doors in the partition are made by gluing together two 6 1/2" × 2 1/4" × 1/16" pieces of balsa wood with a strip of cheesecloth, fine cotton fabric, or typing paper (5/8" × 6") between the layers to function as a hinge. (Commercial dollhouse hinges may be used instead.) Score a "Christian" door design on both sides of the door with a lead pencil. (See Scoring directions under Basic Techniques, page 55.) Put a book or weight on the doors until dry. (Fig. 5) The doorknobs may be fashioned from Sculpey (see Clay Accessories) or wood and glued into place. (Commercial Colonial latches may also be used.)

9. Face the exposed edges of the cardboard doorways with 1/32" thick balsa strips (1/8" wide). (Fig. 6) Sand the edges of the doors with a sandpaper block if they bind.

10. The hinges are glued to the side of the door openings. The door toward the rear is hinged to the left side of the partition and opens into the hall area. The door toward the front is hinged to the right side of the partition and opens into the kitchen. (Fig. 7) This wall unit will fit behind the left-front center post flush with the right side of the post. (Fig. 8) Fit but do not secure.

11. The second downstairs partition next to the steps on the parlor side is made from a piece of cardboard 7 1/2" × 8 7/8", and cut at an angle, as shown in Fig. 9. Fit but do not secure.

12. Next paint both sides of both partitions. I used Hyplar's white gesso for strength and to fill up cracks and irregularities in the cardboard. Gesso looks like a rough plaster finish. Paint the walls of the first floor inside the carton up to a height of 9", where the upstairs floor will be placed.

13. Stain (see Staining directions on page 56) or paint, if you prefer, the doors. Frame the doors with 3/8" × 1/16" balsa or mat board strips, painted or stained to match the doors. (Fig. 10)

14. The steps to the upstairs are made from a strip of lightweight tin, 18 7/8" × 3". This strip is bent to a ninety-degree angle every 7/8". (Fig. 11) Fit but do not secure.

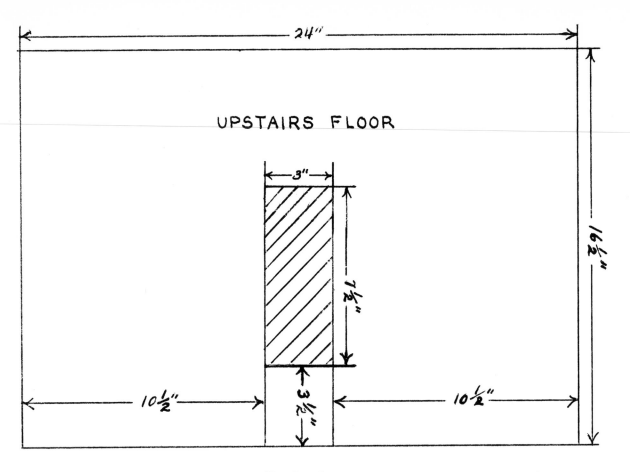

UPSTAIRS FLOOR

FIG. 1

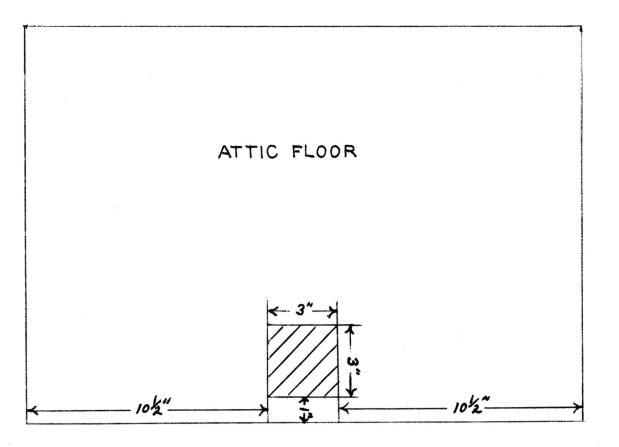

ATTIC FLOOR

FIG. 2

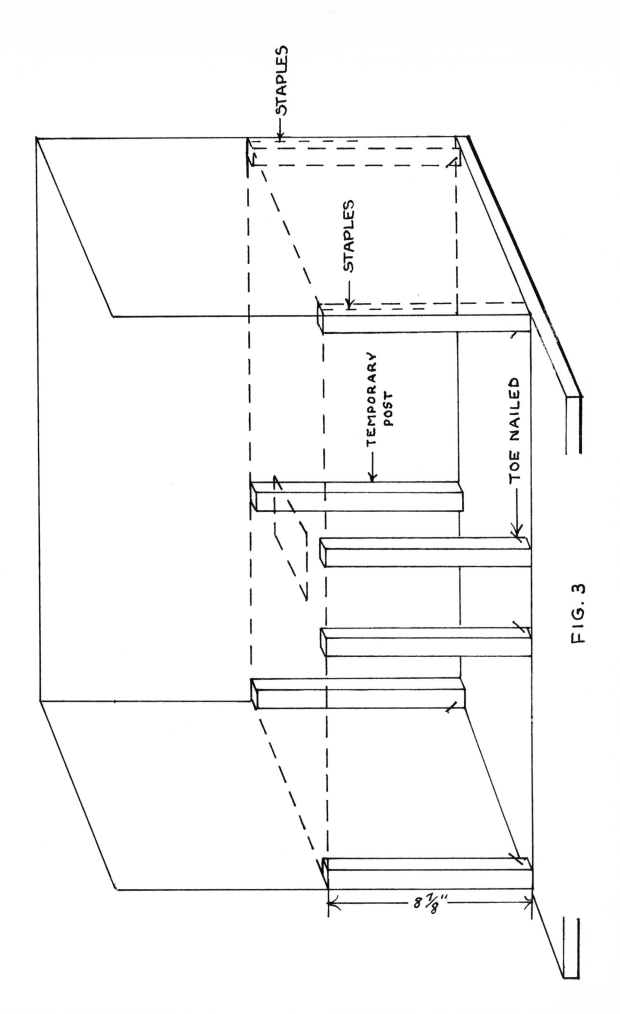

STAPLES

STAPLES

TEMPORARY POST

TOE NAILED

8 7/8"

FIG. 3

9

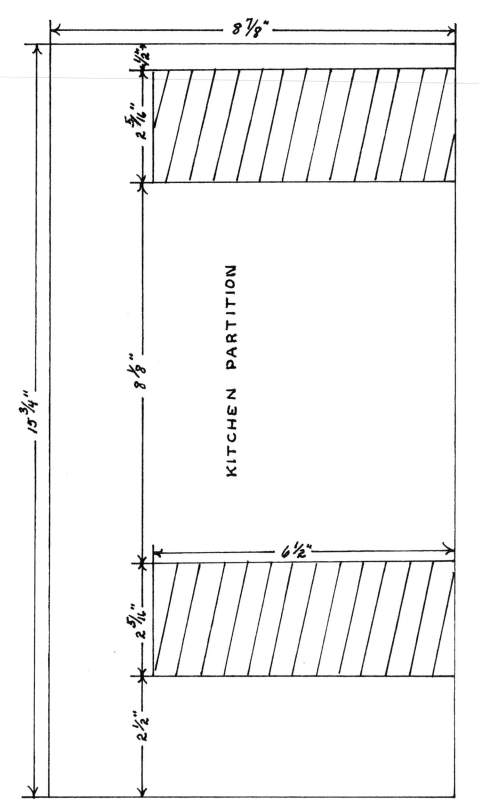

FIG. 4

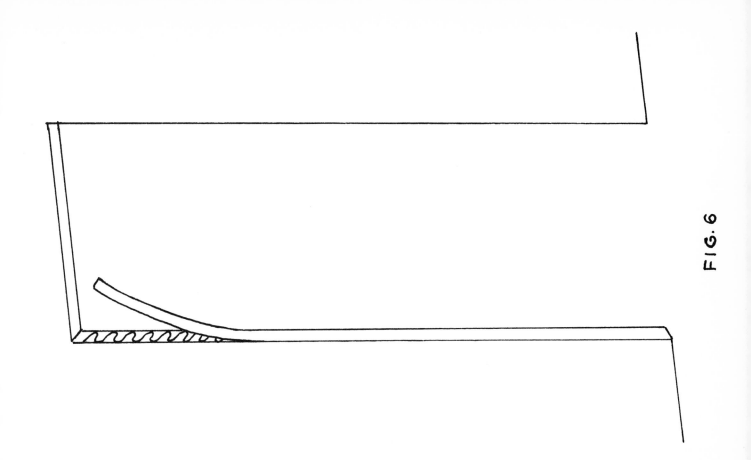

FIG. 6

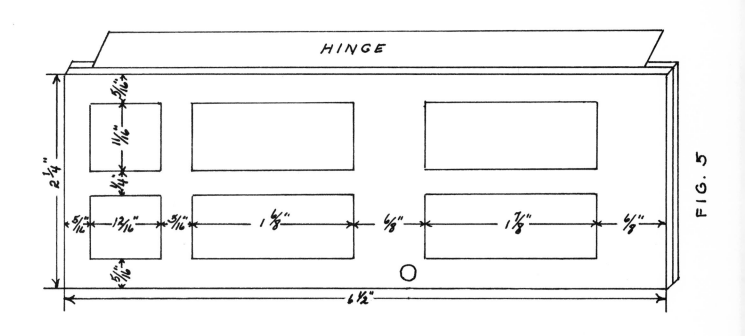

HINGE

FIG. 5

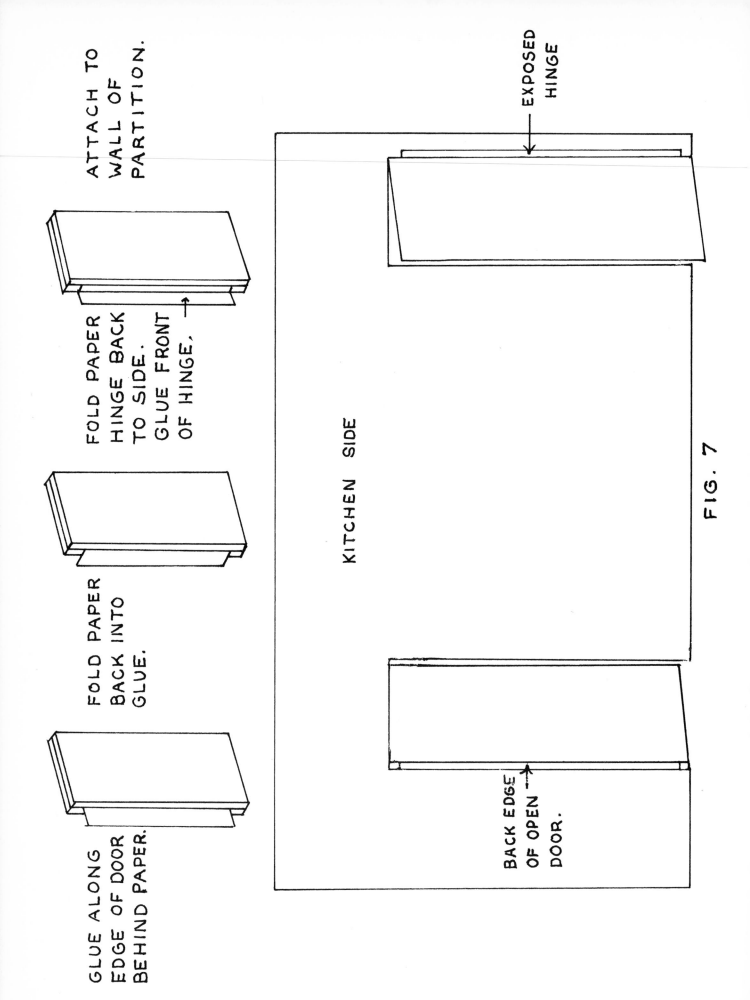

ATTACH TO
WALL OF
PARTITION.

FOLD PAPER
HINGE BACK
TO SIDE.
GLUE FRONT
OF HINGE.

FOLD PAPER
BACK INTO
GLUE.

GLUE ALONG
EDGE OF DOOR
BEHIND PAPER.

EXPOSED
HINGE

KITCHEN SIDE

BACK EDGE
OF OPEN
DOOR.

FIG. 7

KITCHEN AND PARLOR PARTITION

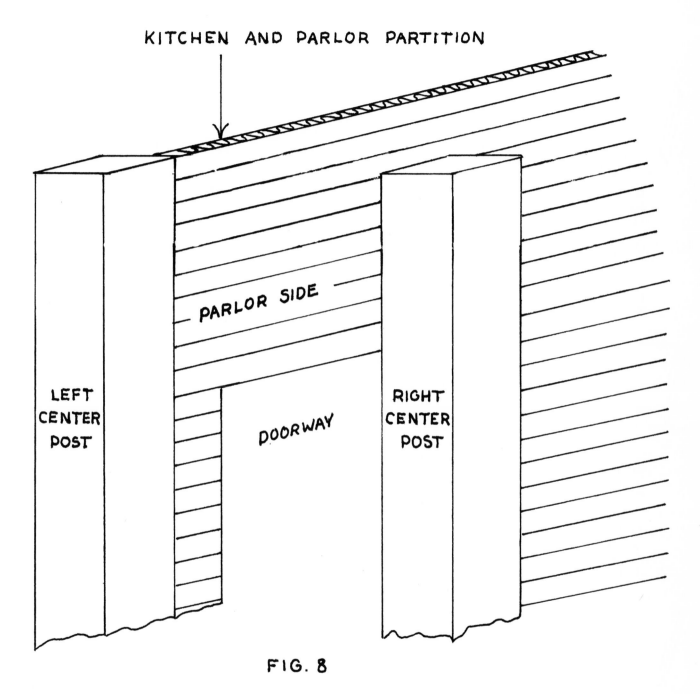

LEFT CENTER POST

PARLOR SIDE

DOORWAY

RIGHT CENTER POST

FIG. 8

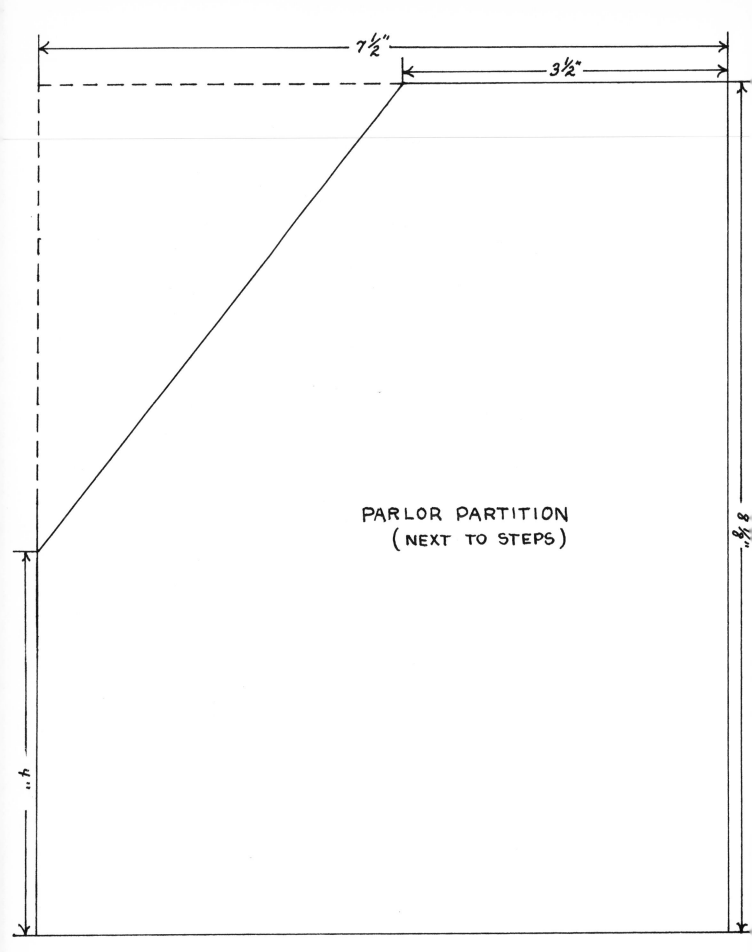

PARLOR PARTITION
(NEXT TO STEPS)

FIG. 9

7½"

3½"

8¼"

4"

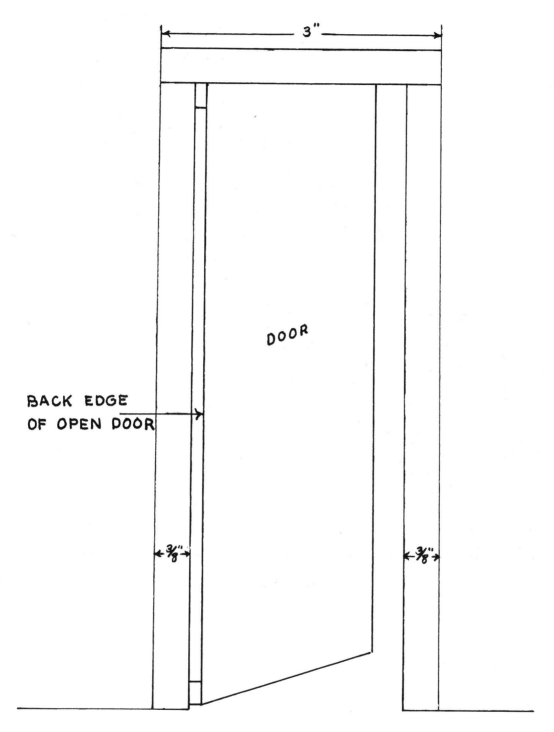

FIG. 10

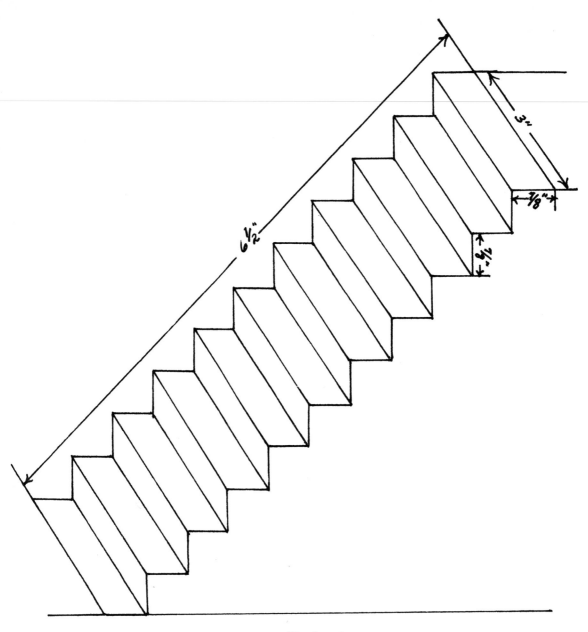

FIG. 11

15. After making sure the steps, partitions, second floor, and keeping room corner post will fit, mark their placement on the floor. Glue the bottom of the keeping room partition to the floor, behind the left front post (see Fig. 8), and against the rear wall.

16. Glue and toenail the stained or painted corner post in the right-hand rear corner of the keeping room.

17. Glue the parlor partition to the floor.

18. Fit, glue, and toenail stained and varnished (or painted) ceiling beams (3/4″ square) between the front upright posts and across the back between the rear kitchen upright posts. Use a heavy back-up metal weight as before. (Fig. 12) After setting nails with the nail punch, fill any holes or cracks with pine crayon stick. (This step is eliminated if you have used shorter 8 1/2″ posts and have already placed the ceiling beams on *top* of the posts, as discussed in Step 5.)

19. Paint the bottom of the second or upstairs floor with white gesso. This will become the downstairs ceiling.

20. Fit and glue stained and varnished (or painted) ceiling beams, 3/4″ × 3/4″ × 10 3/8″, crosswise onto the ceilings of the kitchen and parlor. (Fig. 13) Reinforce the ends by stapling through the top side of the floor into the beams.

21. Glue the top of the posts, ceiling beams and partitions and place the second floor. Put some books on the floor until the glue dries.

22. After a light sanding, the tin steps can be painted. (A drop of liquid soap added to a water-base paint will help the paint to adhere to a slick surface.) Alternately the steps may be covered with contact paper or with fabric glued into place, the latter being my choice. Glue 3/8″ × 6 1/4″ balsa handrail on top of the steps partition. Stain or paint.

23. The steps are secured with glue and mending tape at the top and bottom. The bottom is reinforced with a couple of roofing nails hammered into the floor. These areas are then recovered with another piece of contact paper to hide the nails and tape.

24. Cut a piece of cardboard, 8 7/8″ × 3 1/8″, to enclose the closet area under the steps. Cut a 6″ × 2″ hole for the door. (Fig. 14) The door is constructed using 1/16″ balsa and scored to look like planks or with the "Christian" cross as on the parlor and kitchen doors. (See Fig. 5)

25. Frame the door with 1/4″ strips of mat board or balsa. Stain and varnish (or paint) the door and frame. Paint the area above door (to match the walls and ceiling) with white gesso. Attach hinges to the right side so the door will open into the hall area.

26. Glue the unit to the back edge of the parlor partition (next to steps) and to the ceiling, floor, and the wall partition between the kitchen and the hall area. Tape cracks and corners if necessary, and then repaint.

27. Now you are ready to assemble the upstairs. Cut a piece of cardboard 15 3/4″ × 8 7/8″ for the partition between the bedrooms. Cut a 6 1/2″ × 2 5/16″ hole in this piece for the connecting door. (Fig. 15)

28. Construct the door as before (see Figs. 5 and 14) and hinge to the right side of the bedroom partition. The door will open into the bedroom. Fit but do not secure the partition.

29. The other separating wall is 8 7/8″ × 3 1/4″ and will be placed 5 1/2″ from the bedroom partition to form a small open room at the top of the stairs. Fit but do not secure. (Fig. 16)

30. If you plan to wallpaper the rooms, it is easier to do so now before the partitions are glued into place. I used a small patterned fabric, but commercial wallpaper can be used if you can find an appropriate design. Dollhouse wallpaper is available and bookbinder's paper is also appropriate because it comes in small patterns. Or, you may want to stencil your own designs on the walls, as was sometimes done as a method of decoration in Early-American homes.

Cut the wall covering about 1/2″ larger than necessary and trim any excess later. Use a wallpaper paste because white glue will cause the paper or fabric to stretch as it is applied to the partitions. Use "Yes" paste (a bookbinder's paste) or make your own wheat paste: Mix 3/4 cup flour with enough water to form a thin white saucelike mixture. Heat slowly in a double boiler, stirring constantly. Add small amounts of boiling water to avoid lumps. (Color should be milky-white.) Cool.

If fabric is used, apply paste to wall, then lay fabric on surface. A dry brush or roller is helpful to smooth the paper or fabric into place, moving from the center outward toward the edges. Glue wall covering over edges of the partitions and trim any excess. The walls of the bedrooms should be prepared now as well as the partitions. I did the walls after the windows were cut but this necessitated careful measuring.

31. The stairwell side of the wall partition and the inner walls of the "bath" partition are painted with white modeling paste, to achieve a really rough plaster texture. If you prefer, these walls may be painted with gesso or papered.

32. After the second floor is painted or wallpapered, mark the upstairs floor where the partitions and posts are to be placed.

33. Stain and varnish (or paint) seven posts. (I stained the front of the posts to match the first floor posts and painted the other three sides white to match the doors, molding, and corner posts in the bedrooms.) Glue and toenail these posts in the corners and directly over the doorway posts below. The seventh post will become the corner post in the right-hand rear corner of the blue bedroom. (Note: The upright posts on the second floor may be shortened to 8 1/8″ so that the ceiling beams may rest on top of the posts, as described in Step 5.)

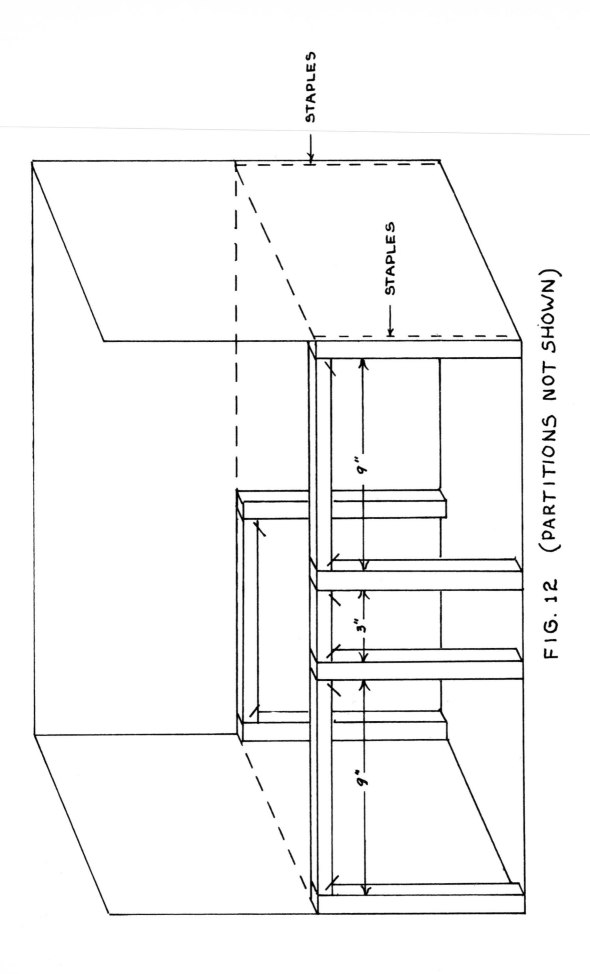

FIG. 12 (PARTITIONS NOT SHOWN)

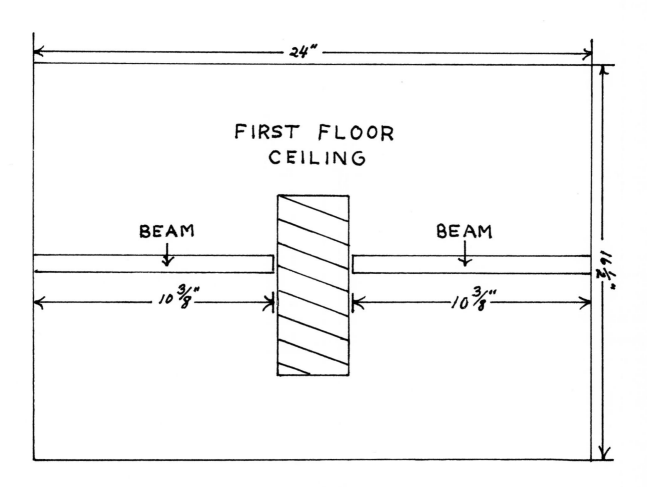

FIG. 13

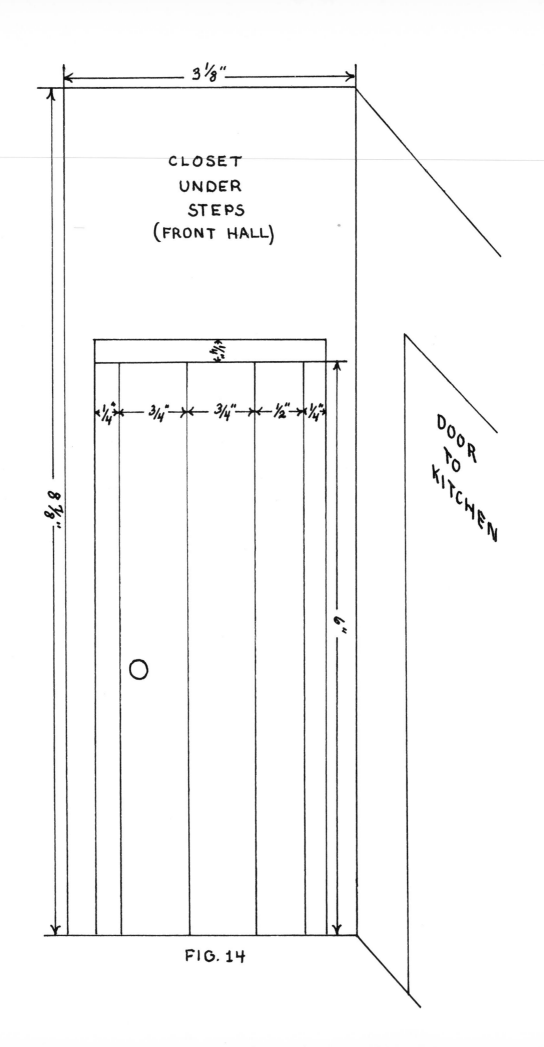

3⅛"

CLOSET
UNDER
STEPS
(FRONT HALL)

¼"

¼" 3/4" 3/4" ½" ¼"

8⅞"

6"

DOOR
TO
KITCHEN

FIG. 14

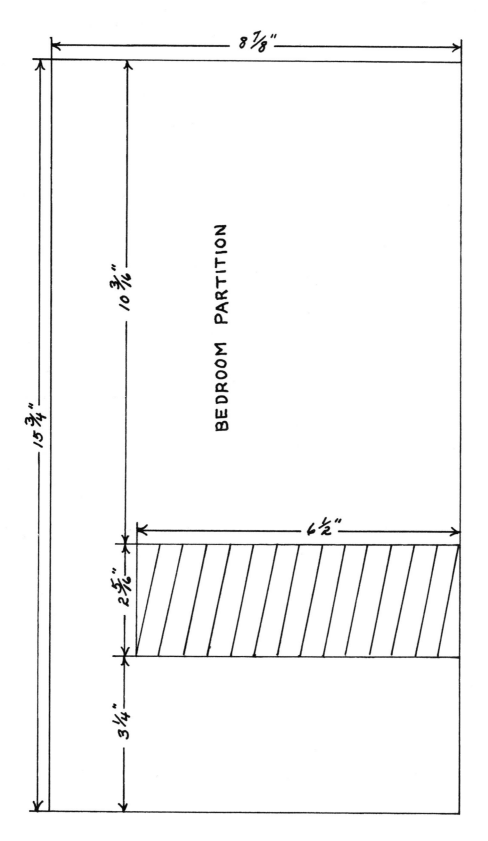

FIG. 15

3 1/4"

8 3/8"

"BATH" PARTITION

FIG. 16

34. Fit, glue, and toenail stained and varnished (or painted) beams across the front between the upright posts and flush in front. (See Fig. 12) (This step is eliminated if you have already placed the ceiling beam on top of shorter posts.) Reinforce corner posts by stapling.

35. Glue partitions where marked on the floor and behind the left front post. (See Fig. 8) Glue and toenail stained or painted post in place in the blue bedroom corner.

36. Cover exposed edges of the cardboard floors, house, and the exposed edge of the "bath" partition with stained and varnished (or painted) balsa strips 1/8" wide by 1/32" thick (*not* mat board). Glue into place.

37. Paint or paper the outside wall of the "bath" area. (The other bedroom walls are already wallpapered.)

38. The upstairs stairwell bannister is added next. Cut two pieces of cardboard, one 7 1/2" × 2 3/4" and another 3" × 2 3/4". Glue these pieces around the stairwell hole and to the wall. The top piece (railing) can be made from mat board or balsa wood 3/8" × 1/16". Glue to the top. (Fig. 17)

39. Make a trap door (with hinges) for the attic floor out of two pieces of 1/16" balsa, each measuring 2 15/16" square. Stain and varnish (or paint). The trap door may have to be sanded if it binds after the exposed edges of the hole in the attic floor are covered with 1/32" strips of balsa. Fasten the hinges of the trap door to the attic floor on the right side and frame (over the hinges and around the hole) with 1/4" mat board or balsa strips. Glue a rope or wooden handle to top. (Fig. 18)

40. Glue the attic floor on top of the posts, beams, and partitions, making sure the trap door is toward the front. Use book weights on top of the floor until the glue dries.

41. Make a ladder for access from the bedroom over the parlor (which I call the "red" bedroom) to the attic out of two pieces of balsa 1/8" × 3/8" × 8 3/4", and eight 2" long pine dowels (1/8" diameter). (Fig. 19) Glue in place at an angle.

42. Cut two pieces of pine 24" × 3/4" × 3/4", and cut two pieces 15" × 3/4" × 3/4". Glue these around the edge of the attic floor. Toenail into the tops of the upstairs corner posts. (Fig. 20) If you have a drill, it is a good idea to drill a hole into the tops of the posts and then nail or screw them together.

43. Make a frame of pine pieces (3/4" × 3/8") to support the roof structure. (Fig. 21a-c) Toenail into the wood circling the attic floor.

44. The roof is made of two pieces of cardboard 26 1/2" × 14". Reinforce each piece 1 3/4" from its bottom edges with one piece of pine 22" × 1/2" × 1/4". Glue and staple pine strip to underside of each half of the roof. Cut a hole measuring 17" × 7 1/2" in one of the roof pieces for access to the attic. (Fig. 22) Cover the exposed edges of the hole with balsa wood.

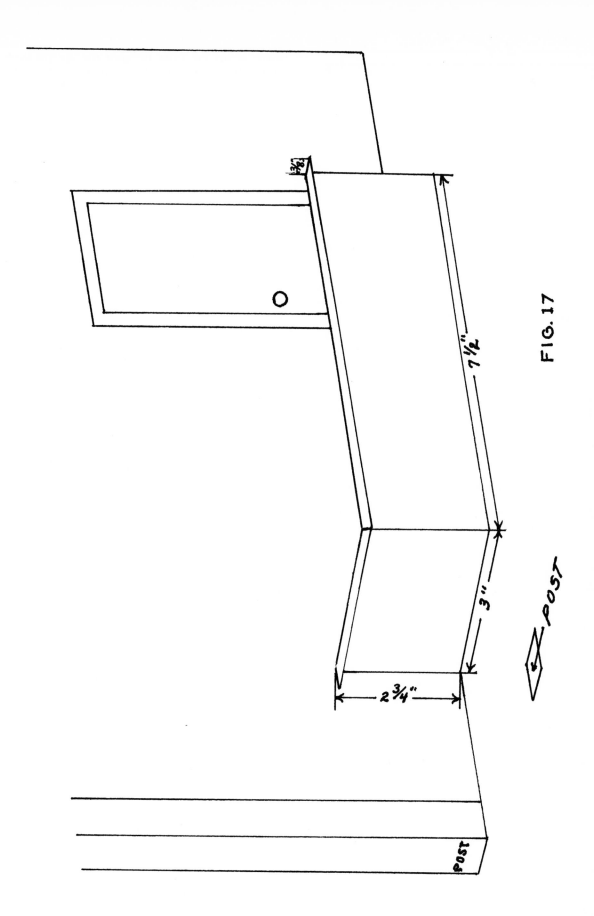

FIG. 17

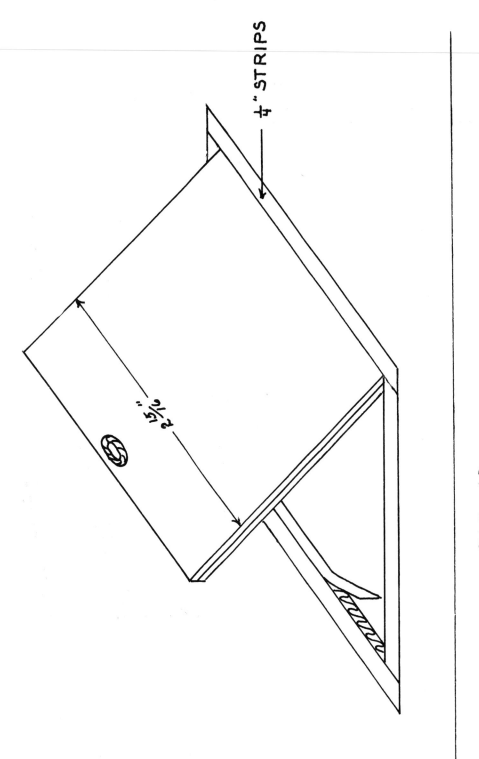

FIG. 18

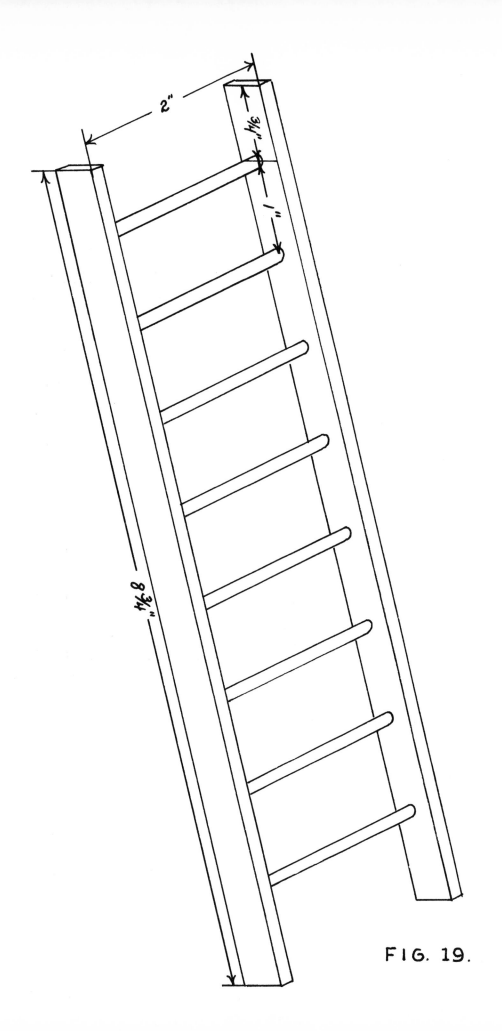

2"

3/4"

1"

8 3/4"

FIG. 19.

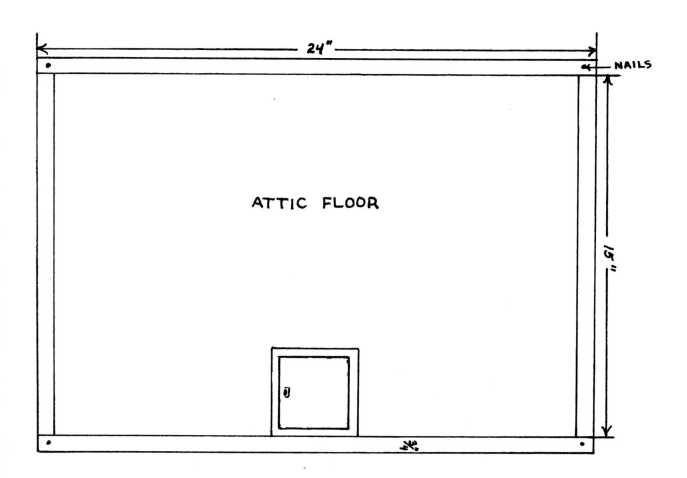

FIG. 20

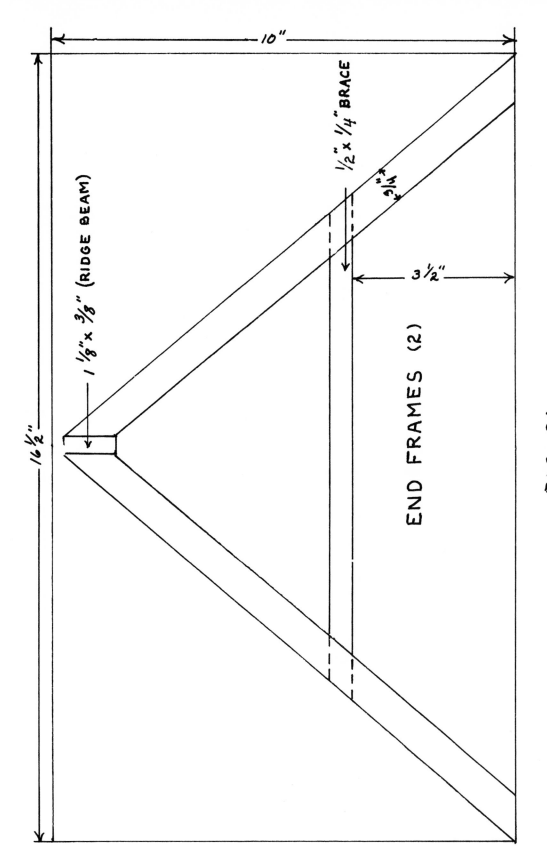

END FRAMES (2)

FIG 21 a.

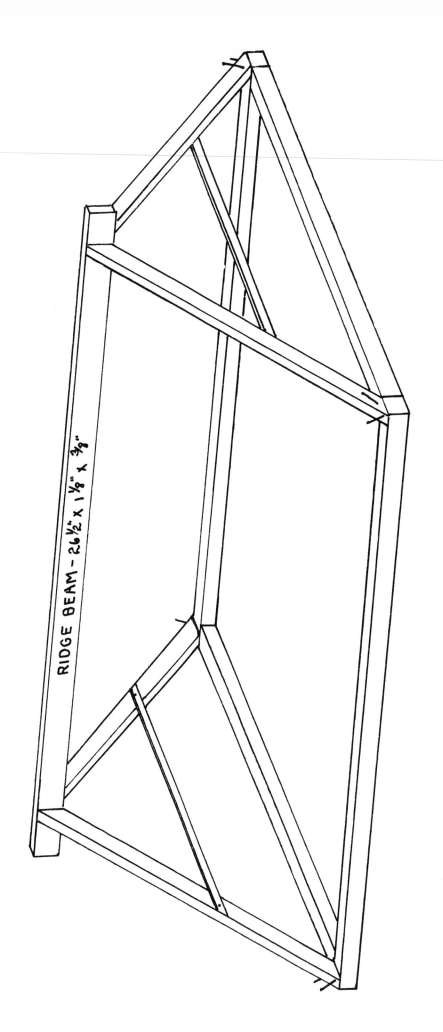

RIDGE BEAM — 26½" x 1½" x ⅜"

FIG. 21 b.

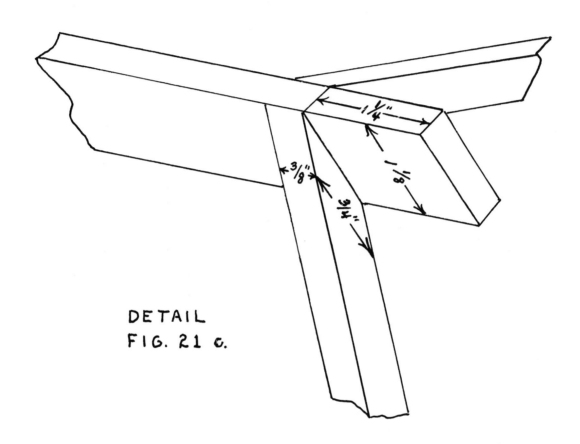

DETAIL
FIG. 21 c.

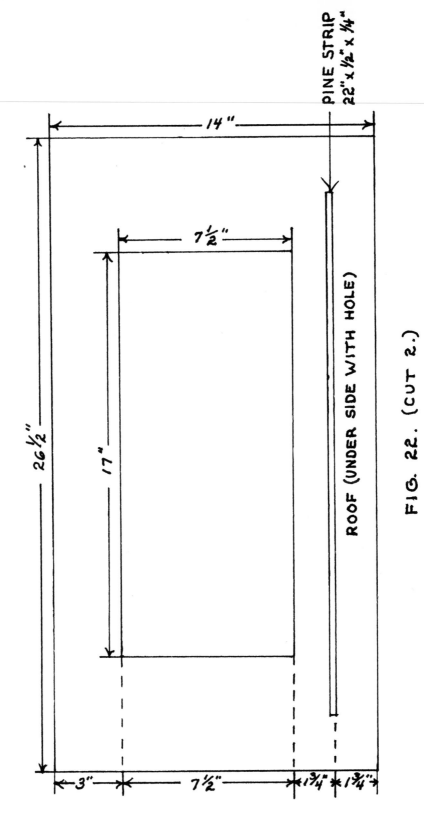

FIG. 22. (CUT 2.)

45. Attach the roof pieces together with tape. Apply some glue on the top of the ridge beam and center the roof in place with the attic hole on the open side of the house. Staple roof to the pine frame underneath. (Fig. 23a, b)

46. Cut two triangular pieces of cardboard to fit under the edge of the roof to complete the sides of the house. (Fig. 24) Staple to the pine end-frames. Tape the connecting cracks.

47. Cut a piece of cardboard 8 1/4" × 9 3/4" for the separating partition. This piece is cut at an angle to fit under the eaves and around the ridge beam. (Fig. 25) Cover exposed edge of the partition. (The room on the left becomes the hired girl's room; the one on the right, the weaving room.)

48. Measure and cut the openings for the windows and front door. Use a sharp knife and be careful not to pull the wall covering loose. (Figs. 26 and 27)

49. Cut two 2 5/8" × 5/8" pieces of mat board or 1/16" balsa for the roof over the front door. Cut another piece 4 1/4" × 5/8" and a triangular piece with a base of 4 1/4" × 1 3/8" altitude to the apex. Glue together. (Fig. 28)

50. Ten overlapping shingles (1" × 5/8") are cut from mat board or 1/16" balsa and glued individually on the roof. Start at the bottom edge and trim top shingles at the peak to fit together. A facing strip 3/16" wide is glued around the front edges of the triangle. (Fig. 29) Glue unit above the door.

51. Cut 56 strips of mat board 26 1/2" × 1" for the roof shingles. (I cut all my shingles individually before I discovered the strip method.) Cut 1/16" wide indentations 1/2" into the edge of the strip every 5/8". Do this for 28 of the strips. Cut indentations into the other 28 strips, starting and ending with 1/4" and having 5/8" spaces in between. You will have to fudge a bit at each end. (Fig. 30) Balsa wood also may be used for the shingles. Cutting the indentations is easier with balsa than with mat board. Dollhouse roofing paper is a third alternative but I like the authentic effect of cut shingles.

52. Line the roof into 1" sections for guidelines. Start gluing the strips at the bottom edge of the roof, overlapping each strip 1/2" and alternating the two kinds of strips cut. (Fig. 31)

53. Cut a strip of mat board (or balsa) 26 1/2" × 1 1/4" for the roof cap. Score the mat board and bend in half to fit the roof peak. (Cut in half if using balsa.) Glue to the peak. (Fig. 32)

54. Paint the roof a gray slate color with acrylic paint. I mixed my own shade of gray using white gesso and a small amount of black acrylic tube paint.

55. The bases for the chimneys and fireplaces are cut from mat board or a sturdy cardboard of about the same weight and thickness. The parlor and blue bedroom fireplaces are made using the same base. (Fig. 33) The red bedroom fireplace is smaller. (Fig. 34) The two attic fireplaces are designed with small rounded openings and the brick is "plastered" over with white modeling paste. (Fig. 35) The kitchen fireplace is the largest and designed for cooking. (Fig. 36) The pattern for the chimneys is shown in Fig. 37.

56. General directions for the fireplaces and chimneys:
a. Cut patterns out of cardboard.
b. Score on dotted lines.
c. Fold on dotted lines.
d. Glue together with white glue and hold the unit together with rubber bands until the glue dries. Tape may be used where necessary.
e. Sculpey, a commercial clay that can be fired in a home oven, may be used to make bricks for a fireplace or chimney. Roll out clay with a rolling pin to a thickness of about 1/8". Cut into individual bricks about 1/2" × 1/8". Make a few bricks 1/4" × 1/8" for the ends. Transfer each brick with tweezers to a cookie tin (or cut them directly on a cookie tin) and bake as directed on the package, (300 degrees F. for 20 minutes). The bricks will turn a brick red color in the baking process and can be used without painting. Cover the fireplace surface with about 1/4" of modeling paste, covering one small area at a time. (Modeling paste is a commercial acrylic product, white in color, but the right consistency for mortar. Add a small amount of black acrylic paint to color it gray.) Set the bricks into the paste with tweezers and allow to dry overnight in a flat position before doing another surface.
f. Another possibility is to set small stones into the mortar to create a stone fireplace.
g. The cardboard may also be covered with dollhouse brick paper or balsa wood which can be scored with a pencil to simulate brick and then painted. (The parlor fireplace is completely covered with balsa wood to create a paneled look. The bedroom fireplaces are paneled with mat board.)
h. The extension above the mantle (inside wall chimney) is not necessary but adds authenticity and can be achieved by adding a box shape on the mantle that reaches to the ceiling. Cover it with brick, wood, or mat-board paneling.
i. The mantle board and decorations to the fireplaces may be fashioned out of balsa wood or mat board.
j. A hearth, made out of cardboard or very thin real slate, may be added to the base. I painted the cardboard a slate color but the hearths could be covered with brick paper if it is used for the main brick construction.
k. Finish the balsa or mat board to match the molding and other wood finish in the house, either stained or painted.

57. The shelves in the kitchen are cut from 1/8" or 1/16" balsa wood. Cut two pieces 6 3/4" × 3/8" for the ends and six pieces 3 3/4" × 3/8" for the shelves. Stain, varnish, or paint and glue the shelves to the end pieces. Glue the unit to the wall. (Fig. 38)

58. The newel post at the bottom of the steps is made from a 3/8" pine dowel. (See Shaping a Leg or Post on page 55) Glue the finished stained and varnished (or painted) post to the floor and the edge of the partition. (Fig. 39)

59. The baseboards around the floors inside the house are made of 3/8" mat board (or balsa). Fit and glue where needed.

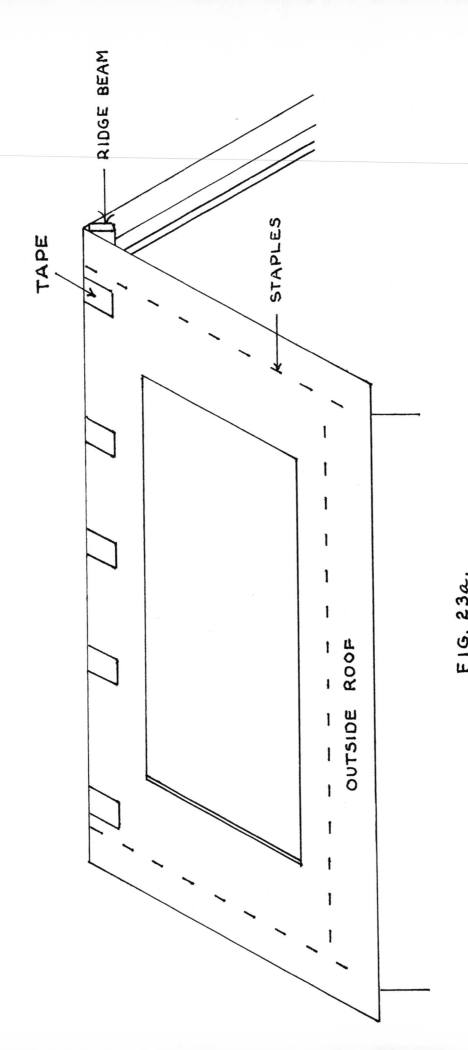

RIDGE BEAM

TAPE

STAPLES

OUTSIDE ROOF

FIG. 23a.

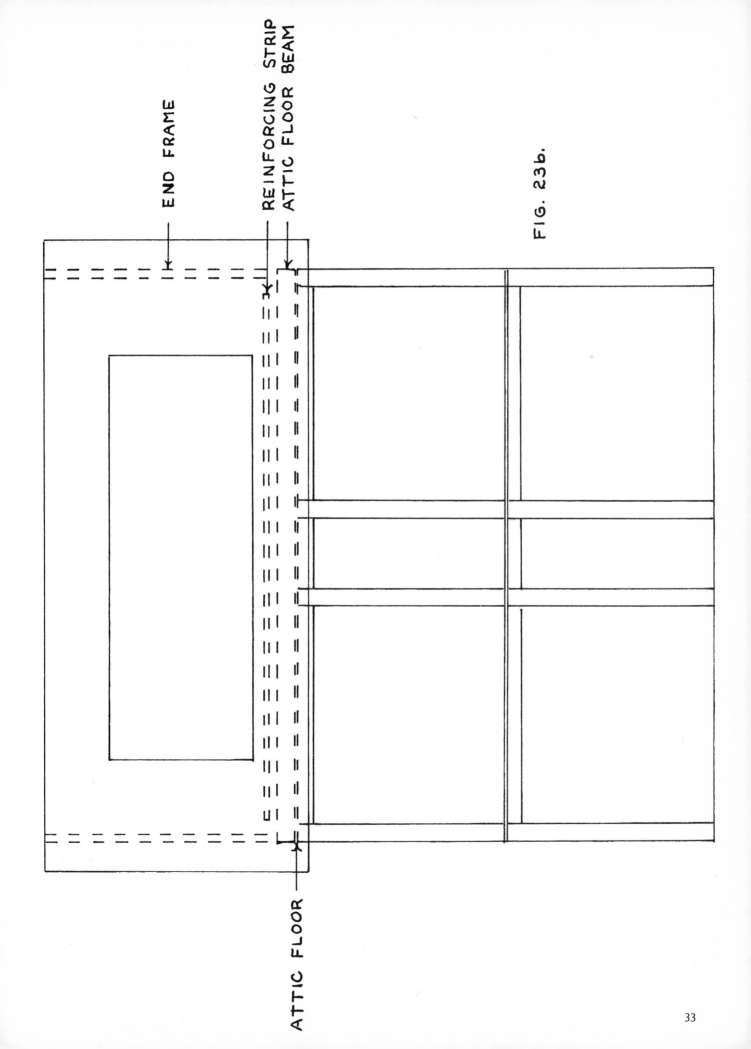

END FRAME

REINFORCING STRIP
ATTIC FLOOR BEAM

ATTIC FLOOR

FIG. 23b.

33

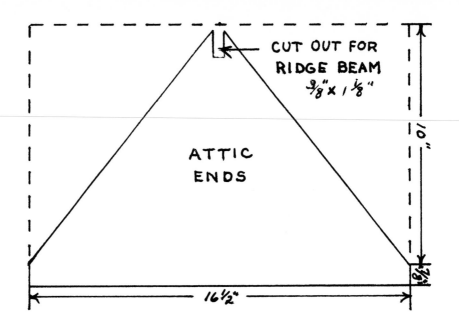

CUT OUT FOR
RIDGE BEAM
$\frac{3}{8}" \times 1\frac{1}{8}"$

ATTIC
ENDS

10"

$\frac{3}{8}"$

16½"

FIG. 24. (CUT 2)

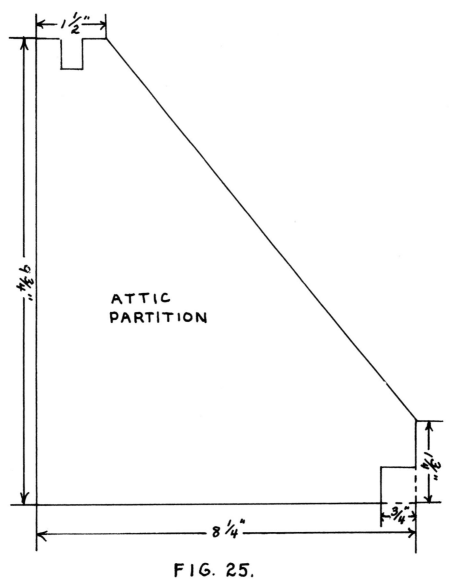

1½"

9¾"

ATTIC
PARTITION

¾"

8¼"

¾"

FIG. 25.

34

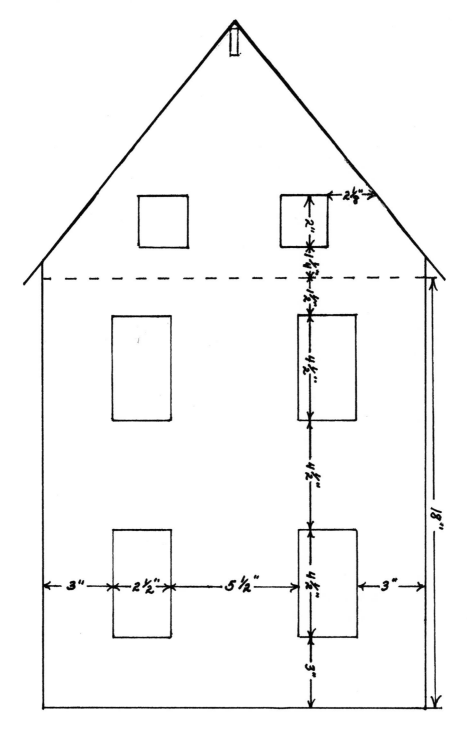

FIG. 26.

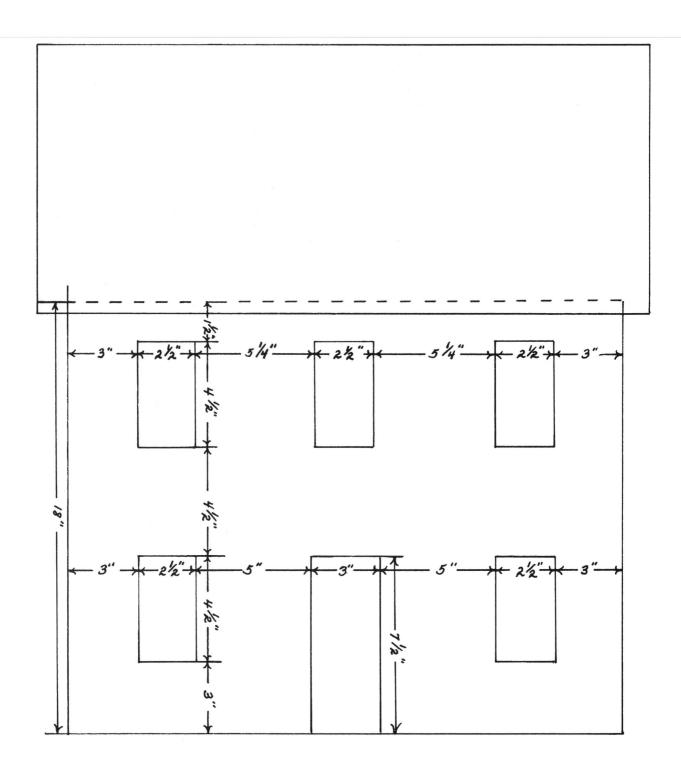

FIG. 27.

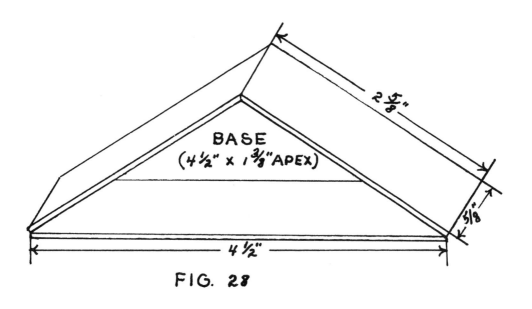

BASE
(4½" x 1⅜"APEX)

2⅝"

⅝"

4½"

FIG. 28

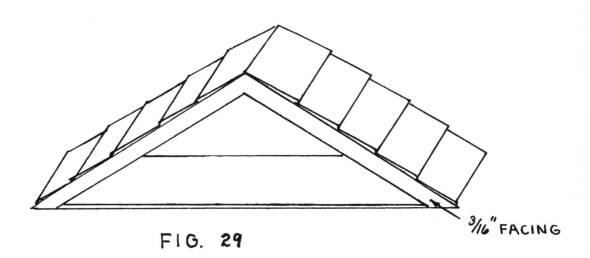

3/16" FACING

FIG. 29

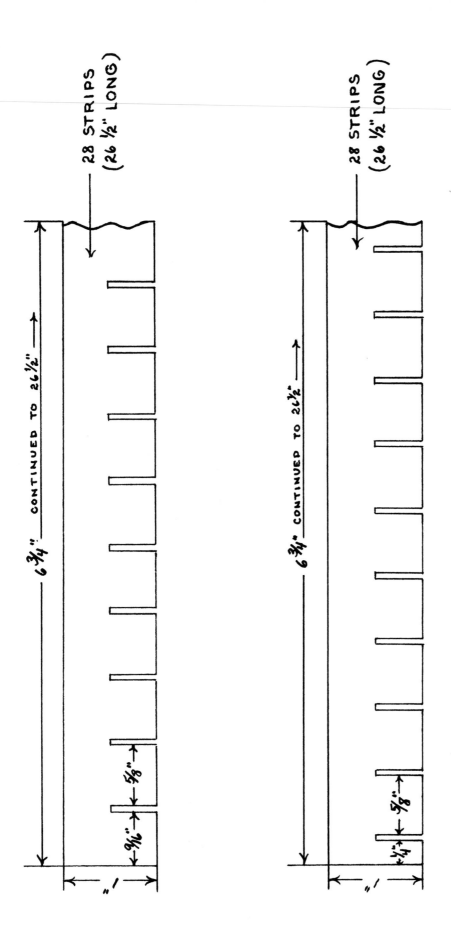

FIG. 30.

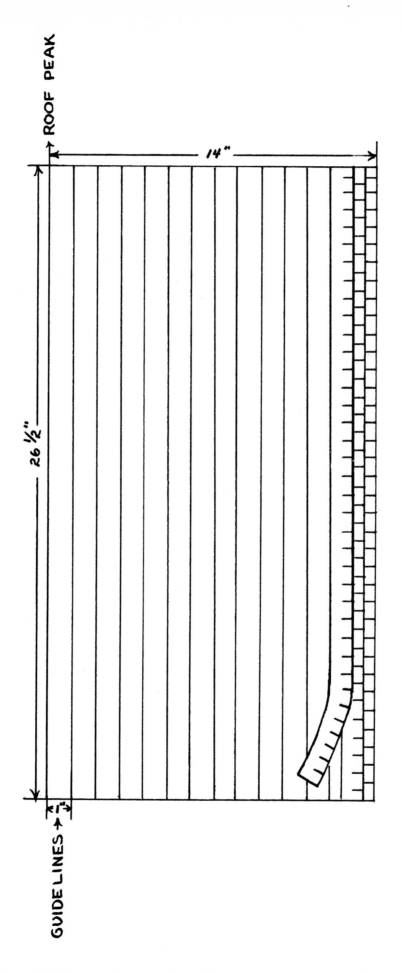

FIG. 31.

39

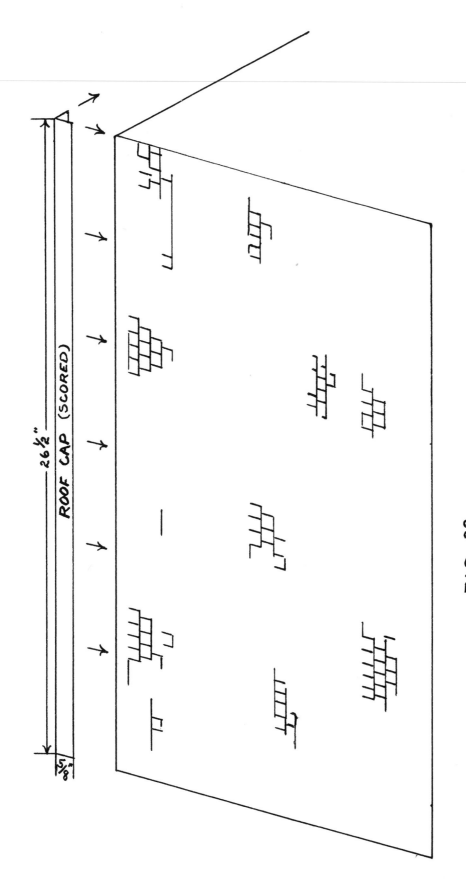

FIG. 32.

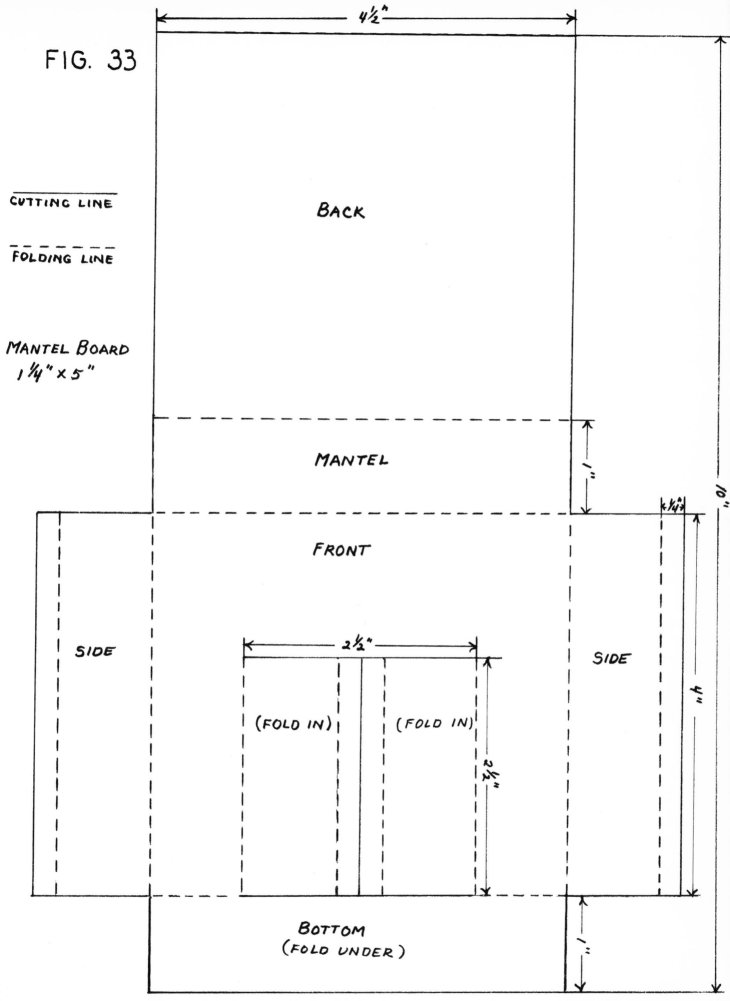

FIG. 33

CUTTING LINE

FOLDING LINE

MANTEL BOARD
1¼" x 5"

4½"

BACK

MANTEL

1"

¼"

FRONT

SIDE

SIDE

4"

2½"

(FOLD IN)

(FOLD IN)

2½"

10"

BOTTOM
(FOLD UNDER)

1"

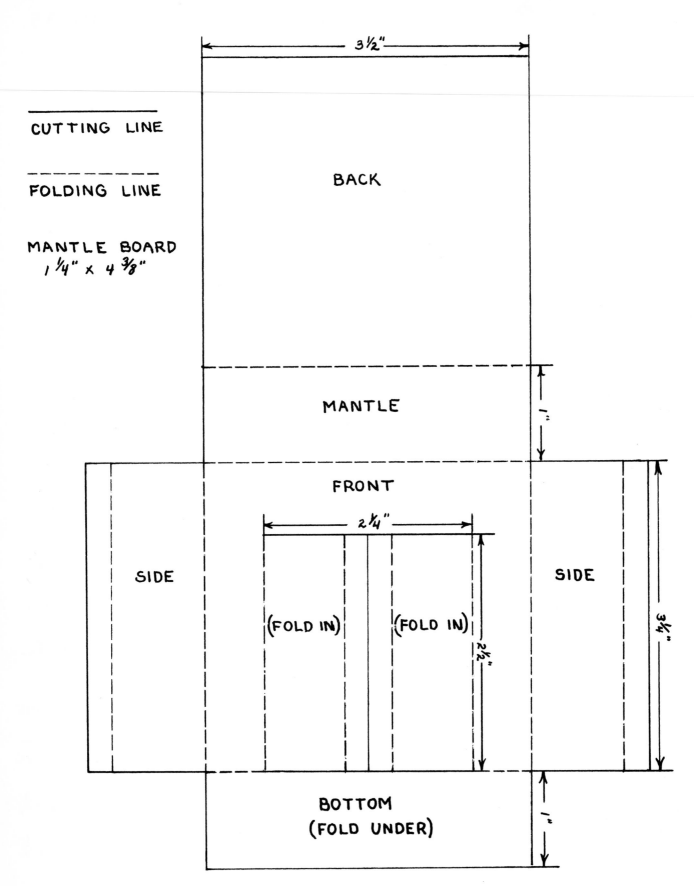

CUTTING LINE

FOLDING LINE

MANTLE BOARD
1 1/4" x 4 3/8"

BACK

MANTLE

FRONT

SIDE

SIDE

(FOLD IN)   (FOLD IN)

BOTTOM
(FOLD UNDER)

3 1/2"

2 1/4"

2 1/2"

3 1/4"

1"

1"

FIG. 34.

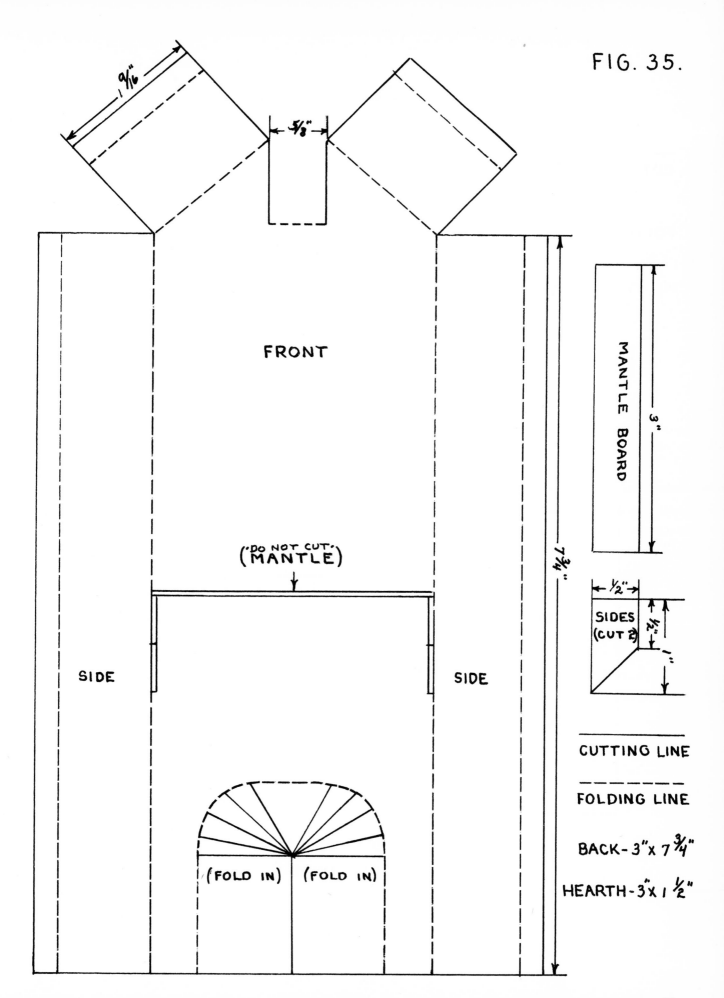

FIG. 35.

9/16"

5/8"

FRONT

MANTLE BOARD

3"

("DO NOT CUT.")
(MANTLE)

7 3/4"

1/2"

SIDES
(CUT 2)

1/2"

1"

SIDE

SIDE

CUTTING LINE

FOLDING LINE

BACK- 3"x 7 3/4"

HEARTH- 3"x 1 1/2"

(FOLD IN)   (FOLD IN)

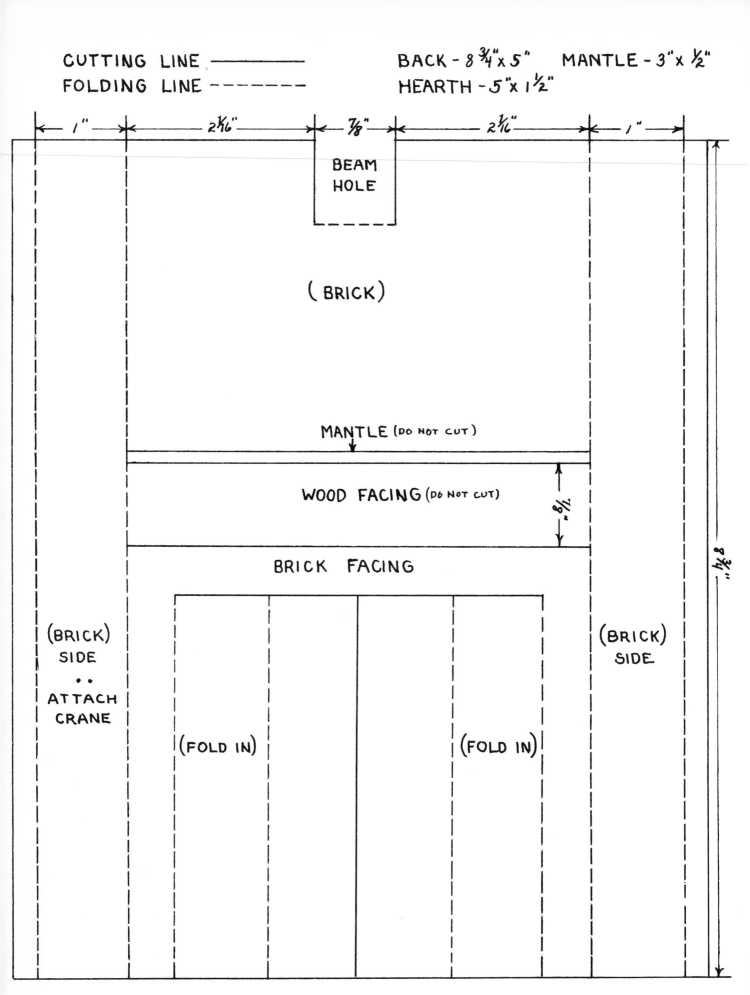

CUTTING LINE ——— BACK - 8¾"x 5" MANTLE - 3"x ½"
FOLDING LINE - - - - HEARTH - 5"x 1½"

1"   2 1/16"   7/8"   2 1/16"   1"

BEAM HOLE

(BRICK)

MANTLE (DO NOT CUT)

WOOD FACING (DO NOT CUT)   ½"

BRICK FACING

(BRICK) SIDE   (BRICK) SIDE

·· ATTACH CRANE

(FOLD IN)   (FOLD IN)

8¾"

FIG. 36.

44

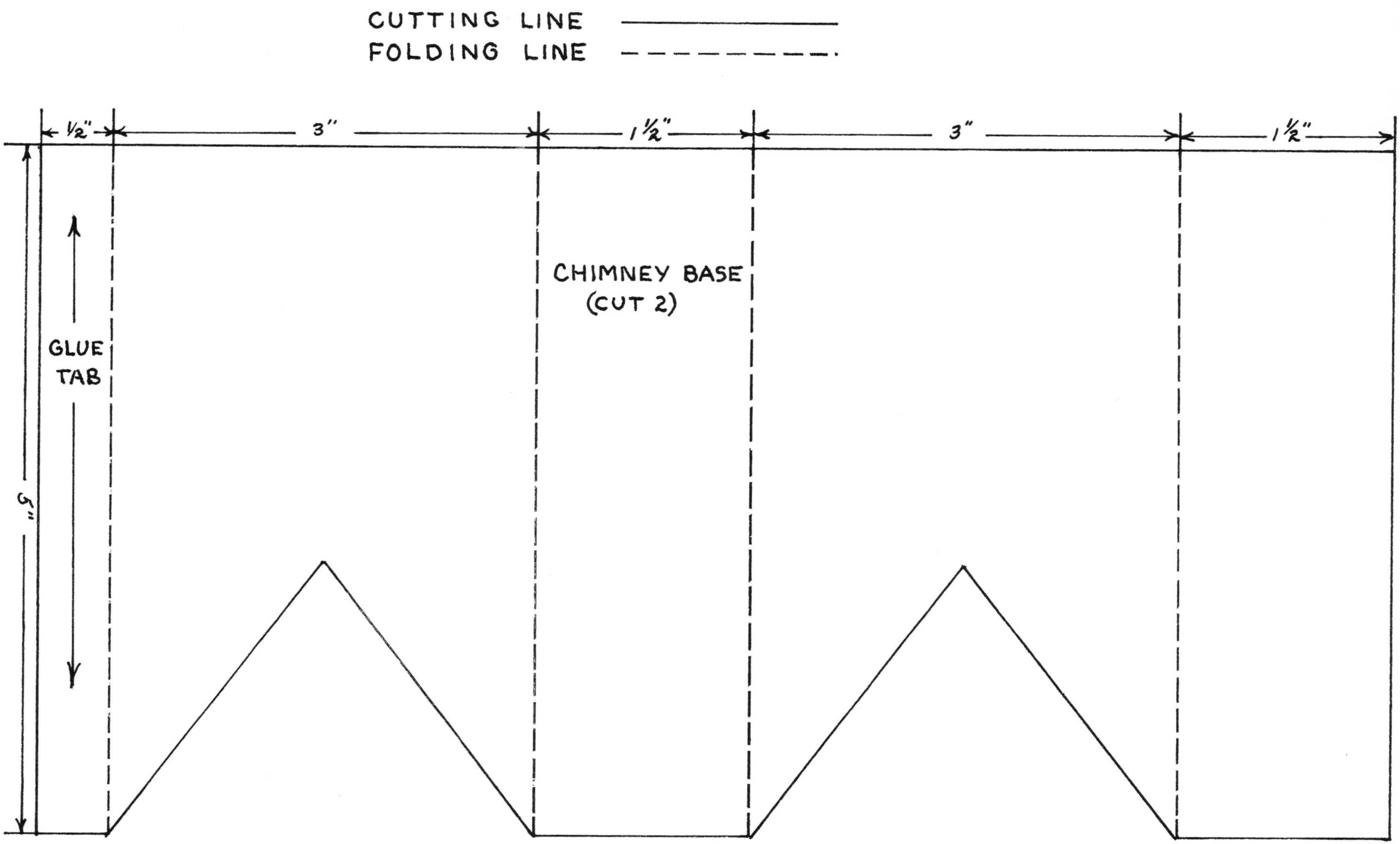

CUTTING LINE ————

FOLDING LINE —·—·—·—

½"

3"

½"

1½"

CHIMNEY BASE
(CUT 2)

3"

½"

GLUE
TAB

5"

3 CHIMNEY POTS – ¾" DIAMETER   CHIMNEY TOP 3"×1½"

FIG. 37.

FIG. 38.

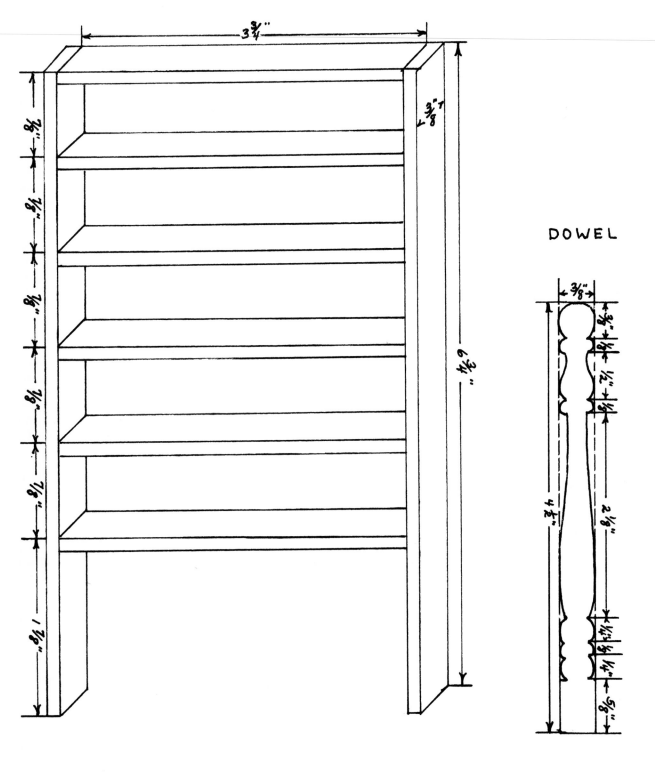

DOWEL

NEWEL POST

FIG. 39.

60. Each of the outside front corners of the house is trimmed with two pieces of mat board 18″ × 1 1/2″ (or four pieces of balsa wood 18″ × 3/4″). Score in the middle lengthwise and glue to the corners on the front. Cut two more pieces of mat board (or balsa) 18″ × 3/4″ to trim the corners on the sides of the house. (No trim is used on the open side of the house, of course.) Glue in place. (Fig. 40)

61. Cut two pieces of mat board (or balsa) 16 1/2″ × 3/4″ for trim below the attic windows. Miter ends to fit roof line. Glue in place. This trim covers the staples on the outside. (See Fig. 40)

62. The edge of the roof is faced with 3/8″ strips of mat board (or balsa) mitered at the corners and glued to the edge.

63. The underside of the roof overhang may be covered with mat board (or balsa) if you wish to add a more finished effect. Cut two pieces 26 1/2″ × 3/4″. Glue and tape to the house and roof.

64. To make the cornices, cut a base 3/4″ × 1″ out of mat board or balsa and trim with 3/8″ sides glued to the base. Glue and tape to the house. (Fig. 41)

65. The "glass" for the windows and door is medium-weight clear plastic that can be purchased in most art stores. Cut 13 pieces 5″ × 3″. The small panes in the windows are simulated by attaching strips of white contact paper (1/8″ wide) to one side of the plastic. Cut four 2 1/2″ square plastic pieces for the attic windows and divide into small panes with contact paper strips as shown in Fig. 42.

66. Glue strips of balsa wood 1/8″ × 1/32″ around the inside edge of the top and two sides of the windows and door opening to cover the exposed cardboard edges. Glue 3/8″ × 1/16″ thick strips of balsa wood on the bottom of windows for the window sills. (Keep edge of sill flush with the outside of the house.) (Fig. 43) Frame the windows and door on the inside with 3/8″ × 1/16″ thick balsa or mat board strips. (See Fig. 10)

67. Use clear-drying epoxy glue to attach the window plastic and the window frames to the outside of the house. Glue the plastic to the house with the contact paper "sashes" on the outside. Frame the outside of the window with 3/8″ mat board (or balsa). (Fig. 44)

68. The Dutch door is made of 1/8″ balsa wood. Cut one piece 3 1/8″ × 2 7/8″ for the lower portion of the door, and another 3 3/4″ × 2 7/8″ for the upper portion. Cut an opening 3″ × 2 1/8″ in upper portion for window. (Cut cross grain first.) Cut a piece of plastic 3 1/4″ × 2 3/8″ and divide into sections with contact paper to simulate small panes as before. For the finishing trim cut 3/8″ × 1/16″ thick balsa strips and glue to the door as shown in Fig. 45, gluing the plastic under the trim in the upper portion and gluing fabric or paper hinges under the trim on *both* parts of the door. (You may prefer to buy commercial miniature hardware for the door.)

69. A small latch, which can be rotated to secure the top and bottom of the door together, is made of balsa wood (5/8″ × 3/16″ × 1/16″) and fastened with a straight pin. Drive the pin through the latch and the door and clip off the exposed shank. (Fig. 46)

70. Cut a door sill 1/2″ square and 3″ long (balsa) and glue to the bottom of the doorway.

71. Attach hinges of Dutch door to right side of doorway. Frame around the outside of the door with 3/8″ strips of mat board (or balsa wood) covering the hinges. (See Fig. 40 for finished effect)

72. Paint the entire outside structure of the house with white gesso. This will fill any cracks and imperfections. Paint the house your preferred color with acrylic paint. The American Eagle over the front door is purchased.

73. Paint the plywood base green or use purchased "grass," available in hobby shops. Ask for miniature train-yard grass. I used this covering but didn't like the color, so I washed it down with an acrylic green of my choice. It gives the yard a nice texture however. You may want to consider using fine sandpaper for grass texture, which can be painted green.

74. The hollyhocks in the garden are plastic and given to me by my friend, Mary Hinckley, who unendingly collects little "goodies." The other flowers in the garden are straw and can be purchased in almost any flower shop or department store. All the herb plants in the herb garden are made from little pieces of sticks and dried pieces of grass and plants from my own yard. I then painted them with acrylic paint to resemble real herbs.

75. The steps to the house and the garden wall are made from "found" stones, which are glued into place around the edges of the plywood base and leading to the doorway entrance.

76. The bird's nest in the eaves is a touch of whimsey I couldn't resist. It is made of dried grasses which are glued together in a circular fashion. The eggs are made of Sculpey. The bird is ceramic.

77. After the house was finished I wanted to illuminate it so that it could be better displayed. To do this I used small Christmas tree lights hidden behind the beams since they didn't have electricity in 1776. I taped and stapled the wire and ran it from floor to floor through small unnoticeable holes in the cardboard floors.

78. To keep the house dust-free and display it safely, I made removable dustcovers out of strips of wood with clear plastic stapled to the frame. These can be screwed onto the house.

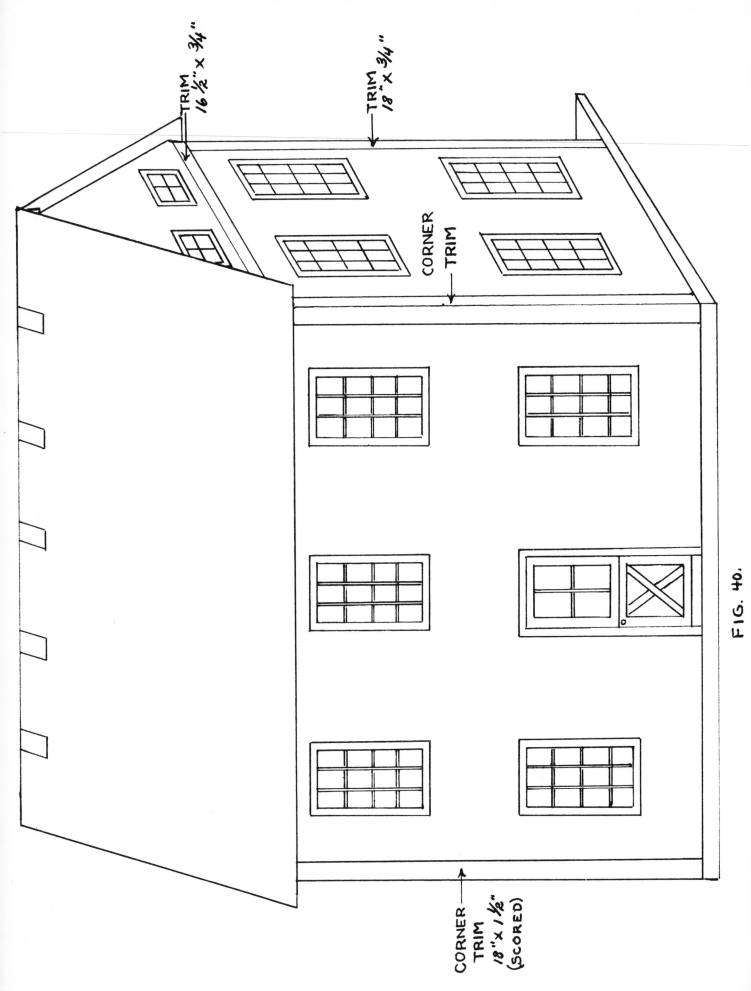

TRIM 16½" × ¾"

TRIM 18" × ¾"

CORNER TRIM

CORNER TRIM 18" × 1½" (SCORED)

FIG. 40.

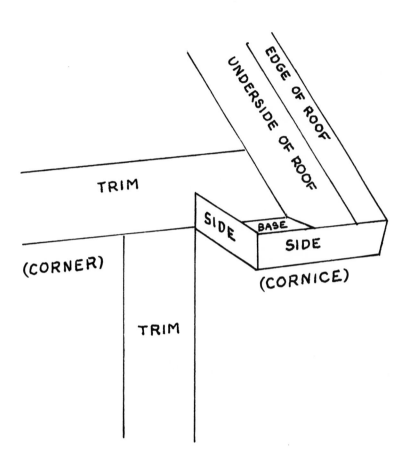

FIG. 41.

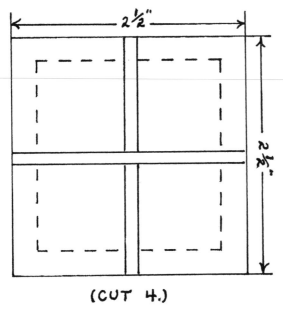

(CUT 4.)

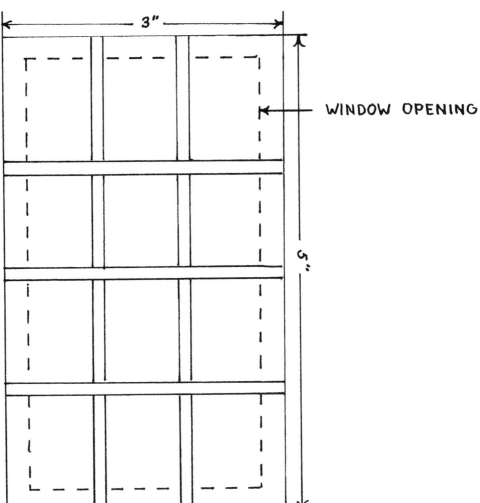

WINDOW OPENING

(CUT 13)

FIG. 42

(INSIDE)

FIG. 43

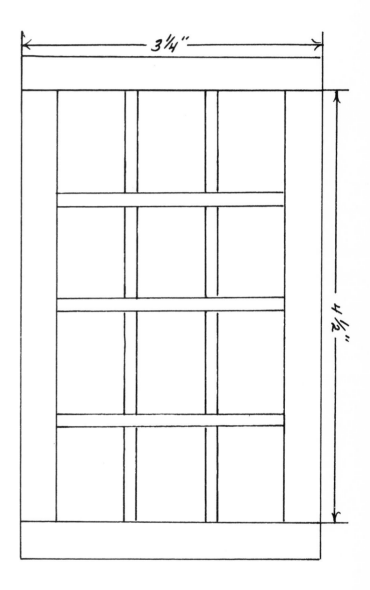

FIG. 44.

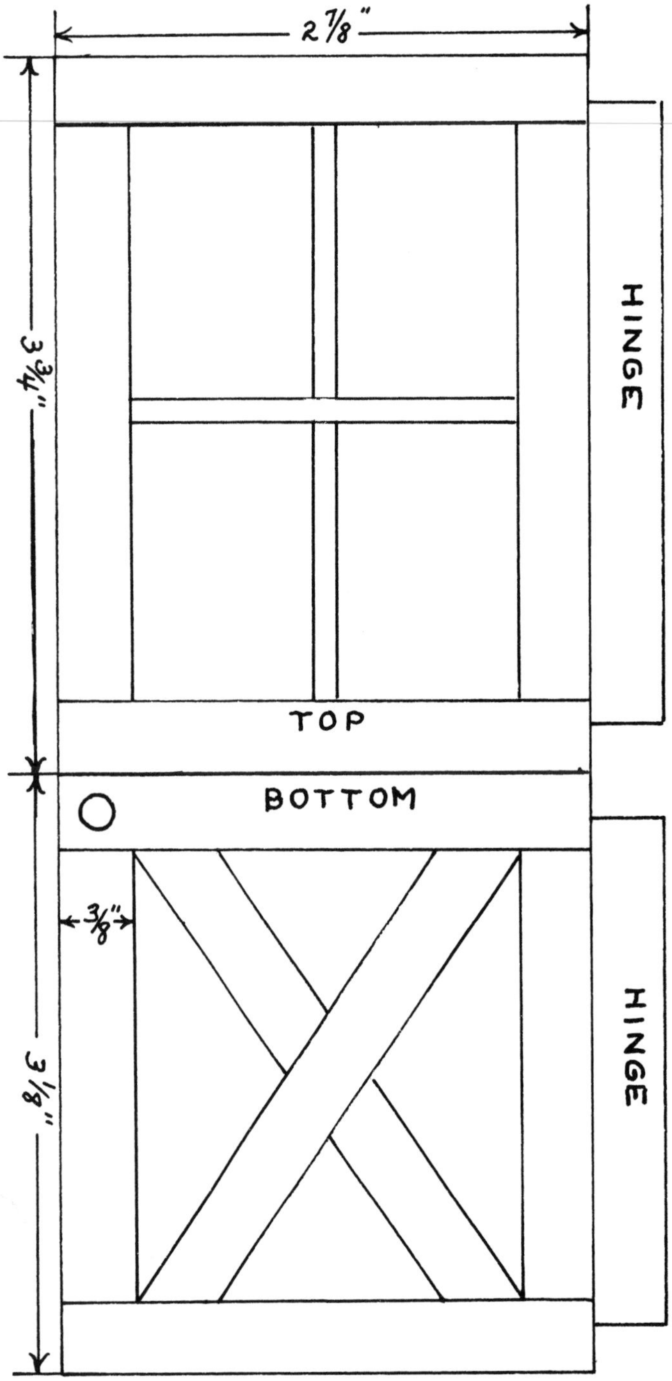

FIG. 45

DUTCH DOOR

2 7/8"

3 3/4"

HINGE

TOP

BOTTOM

3/8"

3 1/8"

HINGE

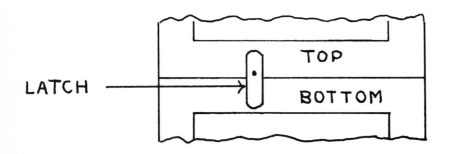

LATCH

TOP

BOTTOM

FIG. 46

INSIDE DUTCH DOOR

Furniture Construction

TOOLS

Many of the basic tools listed below can probably be found in your home. Some miniature equipment will probably have to be purchased. I found that I needed more sophisticated tools when I started using woods harder than balsa. However, everything in the Colonial Dollhouse can be constructed from balsa and, if you are a beginner, I recommend starting with this soft wood.

TOOL LIST FOR BALSA WOOD
Metal-edged ruler (a metal cork-backed ruler is recommended)
X-acto knife handle #1 or #2 or a Stanley knife (if you have one)
X-acto blades #11
Cutting board
Tweezers
Small, round jeweler's file (to make holes in balsa and shape legs)
Scissors
Wood block (for sanding)
Small paint brushes, #8, #10
Small wire-cutting pliers
Miter box (not absolutely necessary but very helpful)
Miniclamps (snap clothespins, rubber bands, hair clips, or U clamps)

TOOL LIST FOR WOODS HARDER THAN BALSA
If you are an advanced beginner and not just starting your adventures in mini-land, you may want to furnish your dollhouse with harder wood pieces. Additional tools are required for working with pine, bass, and hard woods.
Hand saw (X-acto, jeweler's coping saw, or Atlas snap saw)
Jig saw (optional)
Small hand drill and assortment of bits (X-acto pin drill)
Needle-nose pliers
Various shaped files (optional)
Small T-square*
Calipers*
Sequin pins
Small hammer
Plastic angles (30, 45, 60, and 90 degrees) and plastic protractor*

*Helpful when designing your own pieces.

Many craftsmen use dentists' and jewelers' equipment for constructing miniature furniture. Dremel sells an entire line of tools that can be used in miniature work. The Dremel Moto-Shop will saw, sand, and polish, and has a flexible shaft tool with attachments. I invested in the X-acto miter box with a saw and an assortment of X-acto knife blades which fit into several size handles. A miniature lathe is made by Dremel but I do all my wood turnings by hand,

simply because it gives me more satisfaction.

Although many people hand-saw hard woods, it is a tedious job and one which I soon gave up. I purchased a small hobby jig saw from Sears and now I wonder how I got along without it. A hand drill is another necessary tool when working with woods harder than balsa. By using a hand drill, furniture pieces can be joined with dowel joints. This method of construction is sturdier than butting and gluing pieces together, particularly when connecting parts such as chair rungs. However, if you choose to use dowel joints or other types of jointing, the pattern pieces in this book must be adjusted to accommodate the extra length that is necessary to form the connecting parts.

MISCELLANEOUS
Emery boards
Carbon or tracing paper (if you decide to trace the patterns)
Pencil, medium hard with a sharp point for accurate measurements
Sandpaper: 320–400 grit (Tri-Mite), garnet paper is excellent
Steel wool: 0–0000
White Glue: such as Elmer's or clear-drying wood glue (Weldwood)
Stain: acrylic stains (water-base and fast-drying), Min-wax, or other varieties that contain a sealer
Varnish: Val-oil, decoupage finish, or an acrylic varnish
Wood: balsa, pine, bass, or plywoods (for an opaque finish)
"Found" treasures: wood cigar boxes, tongue depressors, swab sticks, toothpicks, lollipop sticks, wooden meat skewers, cocktail picks
Cheesecloth

The patterns in this book may be used interchangeably with balsa or other woods, as long as the wood is the thickness called for in the patterns. Balsa wood is a lightweight wood used by miniature enthusiasts because of the ease with which it can be cut and shaped. You must be gentle with it but it is relatively strong. When purchasing balsa, try to choose those pieces that have tan or brown flecks throughout the length. Avoid those with a pure white color or those that seem unusually soft. Craft stores and art and hobby shops carry a large selection of balsa sizes. The color, softness, pattern of the grain, length, width, and thickness of the wood are things to keep in mind when choosing your pieces. Balsa is commonly available in the following sizes: Length, 36" (sometimes it is packaged in shorter lengths); Widths, 1/8", 3/8", 1/4", 1/2", 1", 3", 4", 6"; Thicknesses, 1/32", 1/16", 3/32", 1/8", 1/4", 1/2", 1", 2"; Square strips, 1/16", 3/32", 1/8", 3/16", 1/4", 1/2". For the following patterns balsa 36" × 4" is recommended, in the thicknesses designated.

The furniture is scaled one inch to the foot. This is the most popular scale used by miniaturists, although many people prefer working with a larger, or even smaller, scale.

Since scale is of the utmost importance in the construction of miniatures, the selection of the wood to be used is of primary concern. Color, uniformity of the grain pattern, strength, and ease in handling should be considered in light of the piece to be constructed. Fine-grained woods are generally desirable. Veneers can often be used. Bass and pine woods are excellent choices and both can be stained effectively to look like other woods. Small woodworking shops will usually accommodate requests for specially milled lumber. Some larger lumber yards carry a limited supply of stock suitable for miniature furniture construction. Craft stores and art and hobby shops sometimes carry bass wood as well as balsa wood. Look in the *Yellow Pages* to find other local sources.

BASIC TECHNIQUES
DESIGNING FURNITURE
If you design your own furniture, you should have a ruler calibrated to various scales (e.g., 1" = 1', 1/2" = 1'). A ruler of this type, usually triangular in shape, and a small T square, calipers, plastic angles, and a protractor can be purchased at office supply stores. These items are inexpensive and will be of invaluable help for accurate measurements. Measure carefully the item you want to reproduce in miniature. Draw patterns *to scale* of the various pieces that will be joined together. Use a fine drawing point. You will find that making cardboard or mat-board models, of the same thickness wood you will be using, will help ensure that the pieces will fit together properly. Working plans (blueprints) of various styles and periods of furniture are available in your library.

TRANSFERRING PATTERNS
The patterns can be transferred to the wood by using tracing paper or carbon paper. You may also cut the pattern out (if it is scaled to size) and draw or cut around it. A drop of rubber cement will hold the pattern in place and will not stain the wood. I prefer to draw the pattern directly onto the wood because it is more precise than tracing. All of the patterns in this book are scaled to size with dimensions given to enable you to transfer the measurements by drawing them directly onto the wood. A small T square or plastic angles are helpful when drawing directly onto the wood.

CUTTING BALSA
It is important when cutting balsa or other thin wood to hold the knife perpendicular to the wood so that the edges will not be angled and will match flush when they are joined together. To cut straight lines, place a metal-edged ruler (as a guide for the knife) on the line to be cut, drawing the blade slowly along the line. Do not use too much pressure or the wood will crush. It is better to make several cuts until you can feel the blade go completely through the wood. Cut the *cross* grain first. (The fibers will run in the direction of the grain.) It is much easier to cut *with* the grain but there is some danger of the wood splitting. Use the same piece of wood for the entire piece of furniture so the grain and the color will be consistent. Make sure you cut the pattern so that the grain is running in the right direction, for strength as well as authenticity. (Think of the "board" construction of the piece you are reproducing.) This is not so important if a piece is made of plywood or if it is to be painted. If you decide to

cut (or saw) individual boards for the back of the settle or the dry sink, instead of scoring the wood to simulate boards, it is advisable to cut or saw all the boards from the same piece of wood in the order that they will be joined together. The boards will then fit together perfectly without cracks. Cut slightly beyond the point where corners meet so as to keep them sharp. Always use a cutting board to prevent marking surfaces underneath your work.

SANDING
Sanding is undertaken throughout the various stages of construction to refine the wood surface. A fine sandpaper is usually applied first and then fine steel wool to achieve a smooth finished surface. Sand lightly, using a wood block covered with sandpaper for flat surfaces. Always sand with the grain direction. An emery board is useful for inside corners and smoothing turned posts.

SHAPING A LEG OR POST
Both square and round wood (dowel) can be used for posts, whichever seems to lend itself better to the turnings. Balsa and bass squares are available. Make a pencil mark where the turning is to be across all sides of a square piece of wood or around a dowel where the pattern indicates, making the ends meet. Cut gently into the line, if using a knife instead of a jeweler's file, for the indentations. Hold the blade perpendicular to the wood until the piece is circled. Then cut at an angle to meet the first line cut so that the chip will fall away. Do not cut too deeply. It is easier to make indentations with various sizes and shapes of jewelers' files but I like to do my initial carving with a knife, as I did for the pieces in the Colonial Dollhouse. Square pieces may be filed all at one time for uniformity, by holding or taping the pieces together as a single block. Trim off the square corners that need to be rounded and the round corners that need to be squared. Taper with a knife where indicated (lower legs) on the patterns. Sand on a sandpaper block by twisting or turning the leg or post. Sand the roughly shaped pieces with emery boards or small strips of emery cloth held around the indentation while turning the leg or post. Curves can also be sanded by wrapping sandpaper around a pencil or dowel that matches the size of the curve.

PINNING A LEG
This procedure provides extra strength but is usually not necessary. First cut off and discard about one-third of a pin, including the head. The pin will fly so this should be done inside a large paper bag. Dip one end of the pin into glue and insert it half-way into the top of the leg. A hole may have to be drilled (see cutting holes in wood below) into the piece before the pin can be inserted. Balsa wood is soft enough to allow the pin to be placed by hand. Dip the other half of the pin into glue, glue the top surface of the leg itself, and insert the pin into the bottom of the chair or table to be joined. Be sure that the pin is straight when it is inserted or the leg will be crooked.

SCORING
Scoring means to cut or indent a groove part-way into a solid surface. Scoring mat board or cardboard part-way with a knife will enable you to bend it precisely along a

straight line. When using a dull pencil to score wood, the groove will be darkened and give the piece a paneled effect or a cut-board effect.

CUTTING HOLES IN WOOD

The easiest way to cut a round hole in balsa wood is to rotate a circular jeweler's file into the wood. Holes in harder wood will have to be drilled with a hand or electric drill, using the correct size bits. (A vise is necessary to hold the piece.) Square or oblong holes are cut with a knife, cross grain first and slightly smaller than indicated on the patterns. Sand the hole with an appropriate size emery board.

BENDING WOOD

Wood has to be softened for bending and then allowed to dry in the desired shape. Soak the wood to be bent in a solution of three parts water to one part ammonia. (Sometimes just soaking it in hot water will be sufficient, depending on the piece and how much it has to be bent.) Be sure the wood is weighted down or taped so that it is immersed and will absorb the water. Soak overnight or until the wood is easily bent. Bend around a form (cans, jars, dowels) that duplicates the desired curve. Tape the wood to the form and allow to dry thoroughly. The color will lighten as it dries.

JOINTING

Jointing refers to how parts are fastened together. Some miniaturists join their pieces by dovetailing, dowel pinning, or tongue and groove. Since I'm not a purist, I use the butt jointing process (solid end flush against solid end) because it is so simple and usually effective for miniature furniture, particularly if joining balsa wood. Harder woods can be reinforced after gluing by using sequin pins for nails where the pieces join. Sequin pins are short straight pins that are used to attach sequins to art objects. They are available in most craft shops. The pin is inserted part-way, the head of the pin is cut off with cutting pliers, and then the remaining shaft is driven in the rest of the way. Remember, the pin head will fly when cut so the procedure should be done inside a large paper bag. The pin may be set farther into the wood with a small nail punch and the hole covered with a wood crayon (found in different wood colors in hardware stores). The patterns in this book are all designed for butt jointing.

MITERING

Mitering is the junction of two pieces of wood at an angle, usually 45 degrees. Picture frames as well as door and window molding are usually mitered at the corners. The X-acto miter box has a straight cut (good for sawing dowels and lengths of wood for legs and such) and two cuts for the opposite 45-degree angles. Place the saw in the desired cut and draw the saw gently toward you. Hold saw handle at the very end and do not bear down. Repeat this backward motion if necessary. Be careful when sawing back and forth or the wood may splinter. There is a lip on the front edge of my miter box to keep it from slipping. If you do not have a plastic angle or miter box, a piece of paper (paper is cut at a 90 degree angle) can be folded to get a 45 degree angle. With the piece of paper flat in front of you, fold so that the top

edge of the paper runs parallel to the left side of the paper. The folded crease will form a 45 degree angle and can be traced onto the wood you want to cut.

MAKING A DRAWER

There are two types of drawer fronts that can be used: The front of a drawer can either fit flush with the front of the piece or can be slightly larger than the hole in which the drawer fits so that the lip acts as a drawer stop. Both kinds are used in the Colonial Dollhouse. If the drawer is to fit flush, it may be cut out of the same piece that is to be used as the front (for example, see the pattern for the blanket chests). The drawer front will then be exactly the same size as the hole where it is to be used. The depth of the drawer must be measured exactly so that the drawer will go all the way to the back of the piece. If not, a drawer stop must be provided.

Use 1/16" stock for the back of the drawer construction. The sides and back rest on the drawer bottom with the side pieces fitted between the front and back pieces. The sides and back should be cut slightly lower than the top of the drawer opening. Drawers have to rest on something, and I have used both runners (strips of wood) and a solid piece of wood to support them. Both are authentic and easy procedures if your measuring is accurate.

Drawer pulls can be made out of slices of pine dowels, pin or nail heads, beads, or shaped from "Sculpey" clay. The pin or nail can be hammered or pushed through the drawer front, the shank clipped in back, and held in place with a spot of glue where it has been clipped. Dowel slices and clay pulls glued in place will be secure enough to allow the drawer to be opened and closed.

GLUING

I prefer to glue pieces together before staining because some corrective sanding may need to be done after gluing and it is very difficult to "touch up" sanded spots with stain. However, this must be done very carefully so that glue is not squeezed out around the joining pieces. Only a very small amount of glue is necessary to hold a unit together. If the glue gets on a part to be stained, wipe it off with a damp cloth and sand over the spot. (Glue is absorbed into the wood and "seals" it so that it will not take the color of a subsequent stain.) Sometimes it is necessary to use miniclamps (see tool list for balsa wood) or weights to hold pieces together to prevent warping until they are dry. Consider carefully the order in which the parts are to be glued together. For instance, a headboard for a bed should be glued separately from the footboard and allowed to dry before the side pieces (rails) are attached. It is a good idea to glue pieces together on wax paper so that excess glue will not adhere the piece to your working surface. (I have glued pieces to my cutting board without realizing it.)

STAINING

Wood stains may be applied with a brush or wiped on with a piece of cloth. (Cheesecloth is best because it is lint-free). Most stains act as a partial sealer. All wood surfaces require sealing. Wood is porous so the little holes in the wood have to be filled to achieve a smooth impregnable surface. Many sealers, particularly stains, will raise the grain in wood (especially balsa) and necessitate light sanding with steel wool. If you stain the parts of a unit *before* gluing them together to avoid glue spots, stain the edges as well as the flat surfaces. Lay the pieces flat to dry so the stain will not run or streak. Wipe with a piece of cheesecloth if the stain is too dark, or wet the cheesecloth in the solvent for the stain and then wipe some of the color away. Allow to dry thoroughly before the varnish or final finish is applied. Stains are available in pine, fruitwood, cherry, maple, walnut, and mahogany, as well as less-known wood colors. I recommend using acrylic stains because they are water-based, fast drying, and are available in small quantites (usually two- and four-ounce quantities) at craft and hobby shops. Eight ounces of stain is more than enough stain to finish all the furniture in the dollhouse.

FINISHING

Val-oil is a combination of oil and varnish and can be used as a final finishing coat as well as a sealer. Each succeeding coat must be sanded lightly with steel wool until the surface is smooth. I like Val-oil because it *penetrates* and seals balsa wood (*after* it is stained the desired shade of wood). Apply Val-oil before painting a balsa piece an opaque color (to strengthen the wood) because paint has a tendency to stay on top of the wood and is not absorbed. There are various stains, colors, and sealers on the market, such as orange or clear shellac, linseed oil, lacquer, wax, opaque colors, and the newer finishes like acrylic, vinyl, or polyurethane. Usually two coats are required to achieve a smooth durable finish. Remember, never use a finish before staining. Remember also that you can put varnish or enamel over lacquer, but never lacquer over paint or varnish. Lacquer will blister whatever finish it covers. Use water to thin water-based paints and acrylic stains. Water-based finishes are odorless, fast-drying, and easy to clean up after use. Oil-based finishes and varnish require turpentine for thinning and clean-up. Thin shellac with alcohol. The product's label will tell you if the paint or finish you want to use is water-based or not. It is not a good idea to use regular watercolors because they sometimes run when the finishing coat is applied. Decoupage finish (aerosol or brush-on) can be used for final finishing. Colorless fingernail polish supplies a high gloss finish for the ceramic pieces. Keep in mind the type of gloss you prefer when choosing varnish for your finishing coat. Varnish can be used over paint or stain for the final coat as long as it is compatible with the base treatment.

Antiquing is another type of finishing that is very effective for miniature furniture (see the Pennsylvania Dutch dower chest in the red bedroom). An antiquing glaze of your color choice can be purchased in small amounts. The glaze is applied over a base paint and then quickly wiped off to let the base color show through. A lint-free cloth, such as cheesecloth, should be used to wipe the glaze. Wipe gently in the direction of the grain and do not wipe too much of the glaze off or you will lose the antique effect. The glaze will stay in corners and cracks and will enhance the antique quality you want to create. Decoupage finish or varnish can be used for the final sealer coat. Always check to see if the finishes you apply are compatible with each other (for instance, use a water-base finish over a water-base paint). Hand-painted decorative finishes should always be protected with a final coat of varnish or plastic spray.

HINGING

Hinges can be simulated by using cheesecloth, fine fabric, or typing paper. Typing paper of good quality is just as strong as a cloth hinge and usually my preference. (See Fig. 7) If hinges are to be used for a box shape with a lid, rather than a door where the exposed hinge is covered with molding, the application is somewhat different. In this case the hinge has to be glued to the underside of the lid (instead of between layers of wood), the back edge of the box unit, and then into the inside of the box. The fabric or paper is folded between the edges of the pieces to be joined. Hinges should be measured 1/4" short of the top and bottom of a door and should be about 5/8" wide. Box hinges may be used in pairs, one on each side of the lid, and should be small in comparison to the piece. Strap hinges (see six-board chest pattern) may be made from fabric, small pieces of thin leather, or, again, typing paper. Strap hinges and butterfly hinges (used on desk) were used extensively during the Colonial period. The hinges are glued to the *outside* of the two pieces you wish to join. Always glue strap hinges with the lid in a closed position. Commercial dollhouse hinges are now available in Colonial designs if you prefer to make this investment. They must be attached with sequin pins.

Furniture Patterns and Directions

In furnishing your dollhouse, you will probably want to construct first the easier pieces such as the wood box, foot stools, and the settles. Progress to the chests and the tables, and finally to the construction of the beds and chairs. The Connecticut slant-top desk-on-frame is probably the most difficult piece to construct.

KEEPING ROOM

In Colonial times, the kitchen, or keeping room, was undoubtedly the busiest part of the house. Cooking was done in the fireplace or on the little black iron frame on the hearth. A swinging wrought iron crane held the pots and kettles over the fire, and, no doubt, a spit was also put into use on occasion.

Dishes, pottery, and cooking implements were often kept on open shelves, as shown here. Closed cupboards, called dressers, came into wider use a little later.

Mother nursed her baby on the "slipper" or "nursing" rocker in the corner and at the same time "slipped" around (without getting up) to attend to other chores. The bottoms of the rockers were often quite flat from this activity.

The Pennsylvania Dutch (German) influence in the Colonial Dollhouse is evident in the beer steins on the mantle and the water bench, as well as in the decorated dower chest in the red bedroom and the "great" chairs in the parlor. The oaken buckets on the water bench were filled with water from the outside well. The chestnut tree was at that time plentiful in Pennsylvania and its wood was popular for household furnishings so perhaps the bride would have brought the chestnut dry sink from there as well.

Colonial furniture was both functional and aesthetically pleasing. You will notice that the child's high chair has splayed legs to avoid tipping. The chair was pulled up to the table and had no tray. The trestle "bord" (in those days a table was referred to as a "bord" since it was usually made from a single pine board) and benches were designed to be taken apart and put aside when not in use. The hutch table (tilt-top) could also be used as a chair, with storage (hutch) under the seat. Some of these pine pieces of furniture might have been handcrafted in one of the woodworking shops in Portsmouth or by itinerant journeymen (often called joiners).

A spice chest and candle box hang on the wall and herbs dry from the beam. It looks as though the lady of the house is in the process of washing her dishes, doesn't it? Take note of the kitty drinking milk and the sampler above the door which reads "Reap Rich Harvests Which Love Has Sown." A Colonial housewife would have taken joy in this pleasant house and, while I wouldn't envy her the lack of electricity and running water, the charm of eighteenth-century homes is something many modern housewives understandably try to emulate.

SLIPPER ROCKER

1. Round corners of seat back.

2. Glue seat back to seat at a slight angle. Edges of both pieces should be beveled for good fit.

3. Glue seat front to *bottom* of seat along front edge. Sand into a rounded shape.

4. Shape back top.

5. Shape and glue two 1 3/8" back posts to middle of rounded indentation in back top.

6. Shape and glue three 1 1/4" back posts between the two longer posts (1 3/8").

7. Shape and glue two 1 5/8" posts to back top, in outside position.

8. Glue the bottoms of all posts to chair seat, the side posts forward on the seat surface and other five posts to the back edge of the seat back.

9. Shape front legs.

10. Cut or saw indentations into bottoms of legs as illustrated.

11. Cut rockers and insert into bottoms of legs at the position indicated on the rocker pattern.

12. Glue side rungs between front and back legs about 1/4" above bottom of legs.

13. Glue top of legs to bottom of chair seat (front legs behind rolled front of seat).

14. Shape and glue front and back rungs between legs about 5/8" above bottom of legs.

15. Paint the chair flat black and decorate back top and seat front with gold paint as illustrated on pattern sheet. Paint ring lines on the posts and legs.

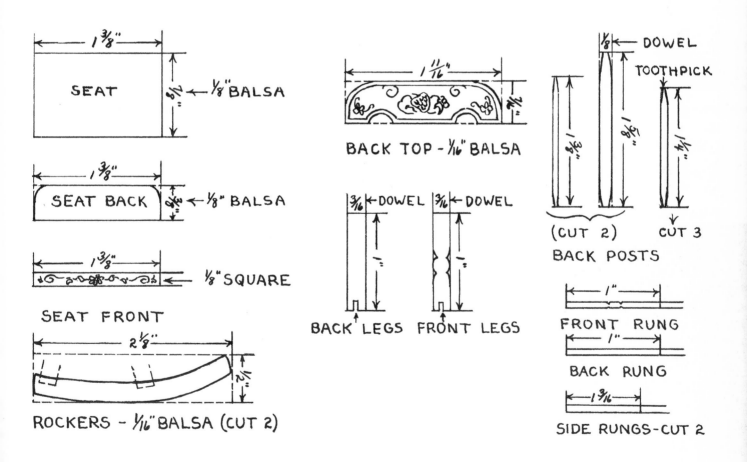

SLIPPER ROCKER

CHILD'S HIGH CHAIR WITH RUSH SEAT

1. Carve rounded finials on tops of back legs.

2. Glue 1" slats, 1" seat rung, and 1" lower rung between the back legs where indicated on pattern sheet.

3. Sand tops of front legs until rounded.

4. Glue 1" seat rung and 1 1/8" front rung between front legs. The front rung should be 1/2" below the seat rung.

5. Allow both front and back units to dry *thoroughly*.

6. Glue 1" arm, 1 1/16" seat, and 1 1/4" lower rungs between front and back units where indicated on the pattern. Hold in place until the glue sets.

7. To rush seat: Cut about a yard of common kitchen string or carpet thread. Fasten the end to left hand rail (rung 1) with glue and clamp with a snap clothespin until dry. Carry cord up through center of chair seat, over and under rung 2, up through center of chair seat again, and back over itself and rung 1. Pass the cord under rung 1 and the first end of the cord. Adjust cord at corner and pull taut. The cord then goes across seat, over and under rung 3, up through center of seat, and over and under rung 2 again. Bring the cord up through center of seat and over to rung 4. Repeat this procedure until you have completed the first round. (Fig. 1) Continue going round the seat in this manner until the seat is filled in. To end weaving carry cord down through the center and tie to any cord on the bottom. When the first rail is longer than the back rail, fill in the corners (Fig. 2) until a square hole is evident, beginning with rung 1 and ending with rung 3. (The ends are glued to rungs 1 and 3 as discussed above.) Continue in the same manner as before to fill in rest of seat.

WATER BENCH

1. Score the back on both sides with a dull-pointed pencil or cut and glue individual boards together.

2. Glue the sides onto the back piece, keeping tops even. Hold in upright position until glue sets.

3. Glue the shelves between the sides and against back where indicated on pattern.

4. Glue top in place.

5. Round edges of top board, if desired.

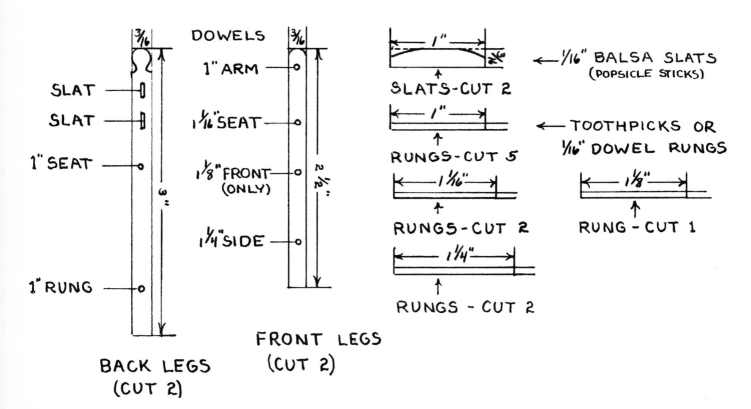

CHILD'S HIGH CHAIR WITH RUSH SEAT

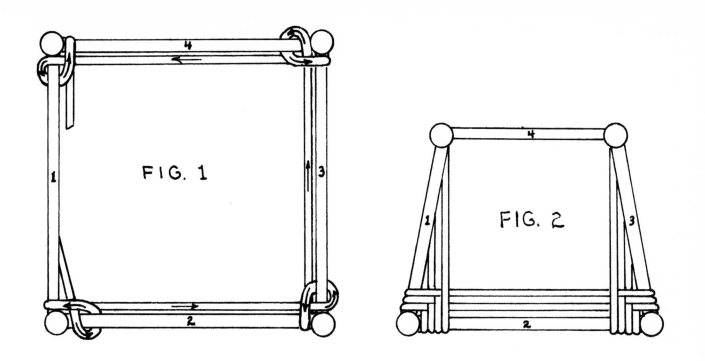

DIRECTIONS FOR RUSH CHAIR SEATS

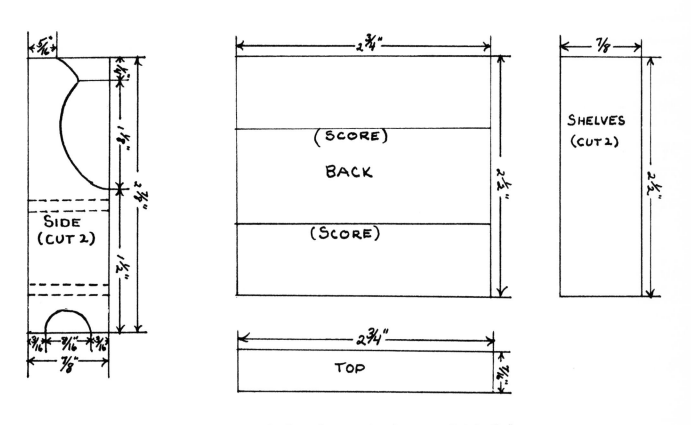

WATER BENCH - ⅛" BALSA

PENNSYLVANIA DUTCH DRY SINK

1. Score back on both sides with dull-pointed pencil, or glue individual boards together.

2. Glue ends to back. Hold in upright position until glue sets.

3. Glue shelves to back and ends where indicated on pattern.

4. Cut doors out of front piece. Score or cut individual front well, side, middle, and lower front leg pieces.

5. Score or carve panels in door fronts as indicated on pattern.

6. Glue front well, side, middle and lower front leg piece in place, if you have not scored these pieces. (The dry-well shelf becomes the counter top and should extend slightly below the front well board so the doors will rest against it when closed.)

7. Hinge doors to front unit.

8. Glue front unit to ends, if boards were not glued individually.

9. Score drawer fronts or make drawers. Add pulls.

10. Glue drawer front piece against ends and top shelf.

11. Glue 1/8" dowel slices to doors for door pulls where indicated on pattern.

12. Attach a wood swivel latch (1/8" × 9/16" × 1/16") with a sequin pin inserted most of the way into the middle board. Clip the excess shank in the rear, leaving just enough to turn over to secure the latch.

13. Paint the well of the dry sink a compatible opaque color.

TRESTLE TABLE WITH BENCHES

1. The top of the table may have two 2 1/2" × 3/16" × 1/8" pieces glued to each end. These pieces are added to trestle tables to prevent splitting and warping of the table board, but are not necessary on a miniature-sized model.

2. Drill 1/8" holes in the trestle boards and cut holes in table ends.

3. Glue table braces onto the underside of table top. The first brace will be 3/4" from the end (or 1" if you have used extension pieces). Glue another brace 1/8" (plus a bit) from the first one toward the center of the table. Repeat at the other end. The table ends should fit between the braces. This style of table was designed to be taken apart and put aside when not in use.

4. Insert trestle board through holes in table ends and secure with pine dowels. The holes may have to be sanded a bit to accommodate the trestle board. The dowels may have to be gently forced through the holes in the trestle board the first time.

5. Glue the bench braces to the underside of the bench tops the same as table but place the first brace 3/8" from the end. Secure bench trestle boards to the bench ends with pegs as before.

6. Sand the ends of the table and bench feet until rounded.

7. Glue the feet to the end pieces, centered for stability.

HUTCH TABLE

1. Drill 1/8" holes in side pieces and table braces where indicated on pattern.

2. Glue short edges (1 3/8") of the seat bottom between the sides where indicated on pattern.

3. Glue the front and back panels on top of the seat bottom and against the sides.

4. Attach the seat top with hinges. The seat will extend in front as shown on pattern.

5. Score top on both sides with a pencil, or glue individual boards together. Top size is optional.

6. Glue table braces at right angles to the boards as shown on pattern, making sure the braces will be on the *outside* of the chair sides.

7. Cut two 5/8" lengths of 1/8" dowel for pegs to attach the table top to the chair. The pegs will have to be gently forced into the holes the first few times.

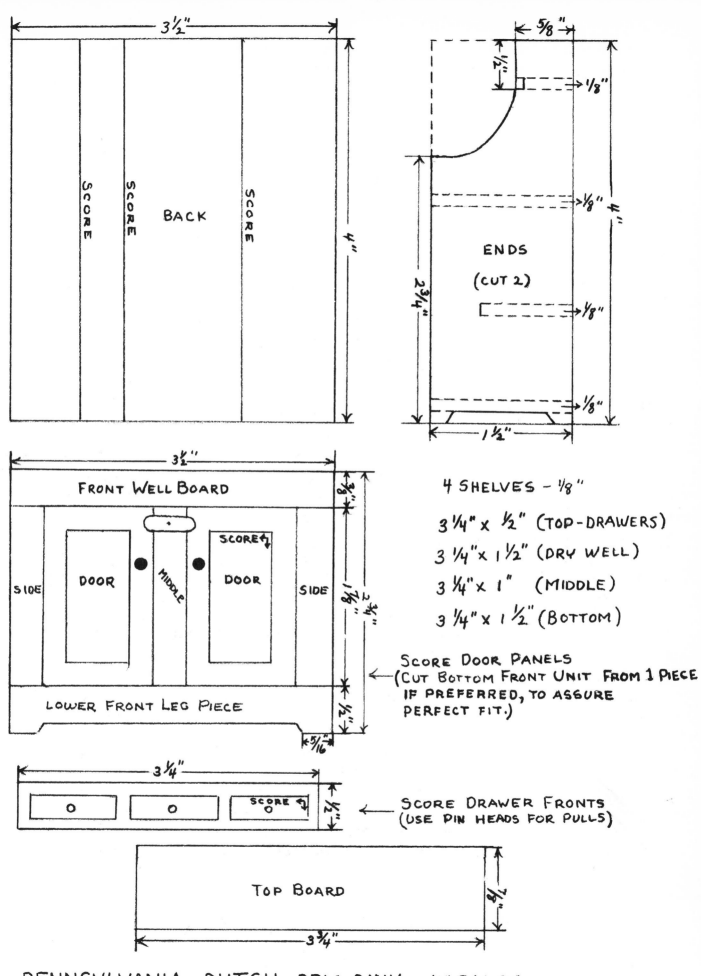

3½"

SCORE SCORE BACK SCORE

4"

5/8"

¼"

⅛"

ENDS
(CUT 2)

4"

2¾"

⅛"

⅛"

1½"

3½"

FRONT WELL BOARD

3/8"

SCORE

SIDE DOOR MIDDLE DOOR SIDE

1⅛"

2¾"

LOWER FRONT LEG PIECE

½"

5/16"

4 SHELVES – ⅛"

3¼" x ½" (TOP-DRAWERS)

3¼" x 1½" (DRY WELL)

3¼" x 1" (MIDDLE)

3¼" x 1½" (BOTTOM)

SCORE DOOR PANELS
(CUT BOTTOM FRONT UNIT FROM 1 PIECE
IF PREFERRED, TO ASSURE
PERFECT FIT.)

3¼"

SCORE

½"

SCORE DRAWER FRONTS
(USE PIN HEADS FOR PULLS)

TOP BOARD

½"

3¾"

PENNSYLVANIA DUTCH DRY SINK – ⅛" BALSA

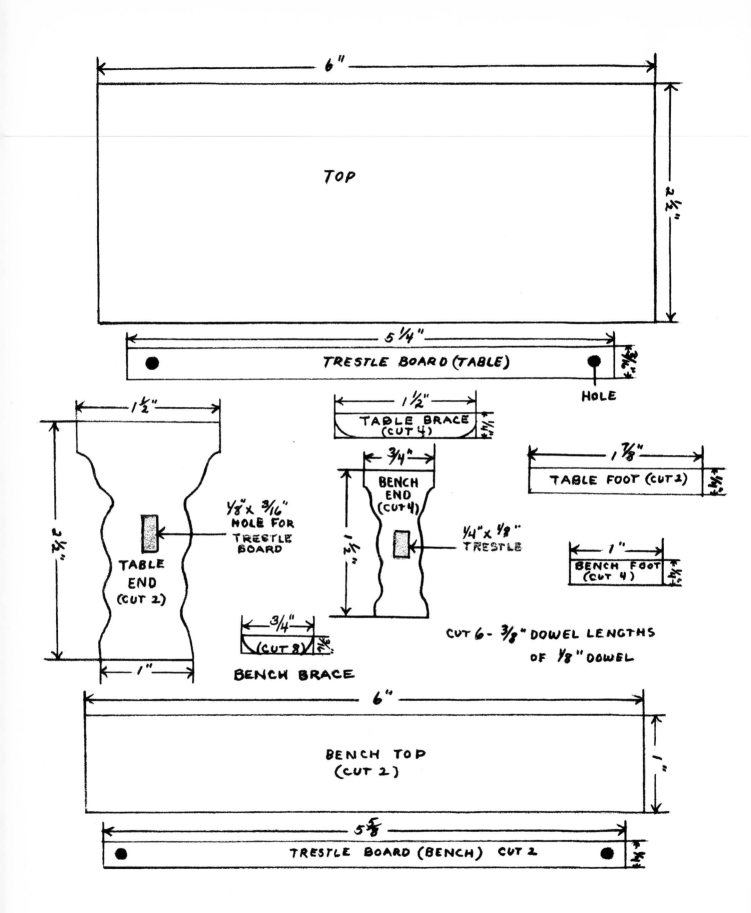

TOP

6"

2½"

TRESTLE BOARD (TABLE)

5¼"

HOLE

TABLE END (CUT 2)

1½"

2½"

1"

⅛"x 3/16" HOLE FOR TRESTLE BOARD

TABLE BRACE (CUT 4)

1½"

BENCH END (CUT 4)

¾"

1½"

¼"x ⅛" TRESTLE

TABLE FOOT (CUT 2)

1⅞"

BENCH FOOT (CUT 4)

1"

CUT 6 - ⅜" DOWEL LENGTHS OF ⅛" DOWEL

BENCH BRACE

¾"

(CUT 8)

BENCH TOP (CUT 2)

6"

1"

TRESTLE BOARD (BENCH) CUT 2

5⅝"

TRESTLE TABLE WITH BENCHES
⅛" BALSA

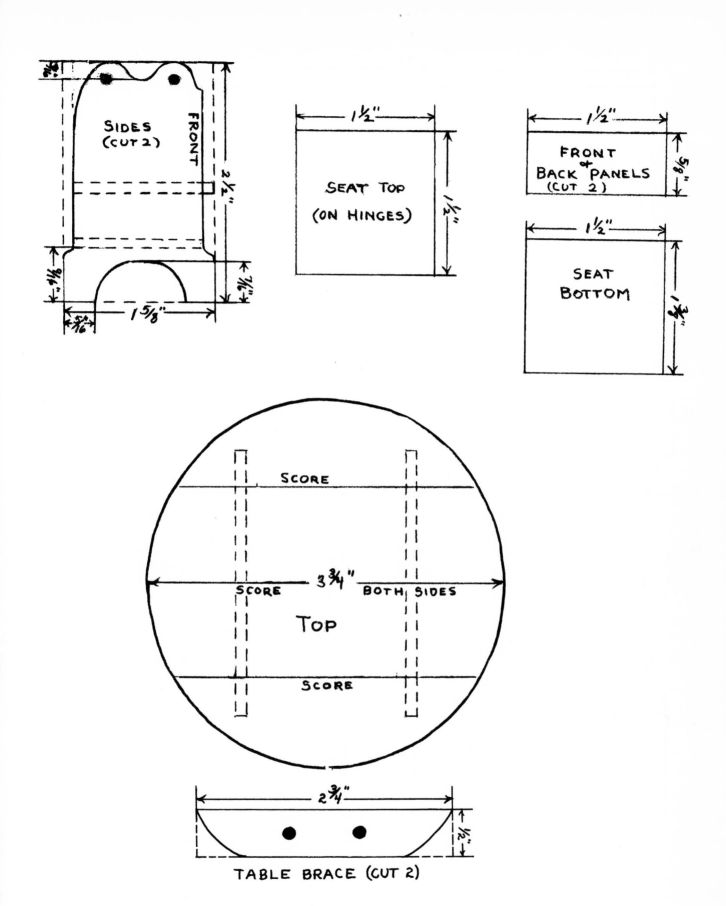

SIDES
(CUT 2)

FRONT

2½"

1⁵⁄₈"

SEAT TOP
(ON HINGES)

1½"

1½"

FRONT
&
BACK PANELS
(CUT 2)

1½"

⅝"

SEAT
BOTTOM

1½"

¾"

SCORE

SCORE

3¾"

BOTH SIDES

TOP

SCORE

2¾"

½"

TABLE BRACE (CUT 2)

HUTCH TABLE - ⅛" (⅛"PEGS)

PARLOR

Furniture items like the Chippendale wing chair with ball feet, Chippendale mantle clock, and Connecticut desk-on-frame could have been purchased in Boston, about fifty-five miles from Portsmouth. (Chippendale, an eighteenth-century English cabinetmaker, had made his designs available to American cabinetmakers in 1754 through his publication *Gentleman and Cabinet Maker's Director*.) The desk has a slant top with butterfly hinges. The first desks were just boxes set on tables for writing or reading. They were often fitted with a strip of molding to hold the book or paper on the slanted top. When the desk top was mounted on legs, the base stretcher was moved back to allow leg room for comfortable sitting. Many desks had a drawer either in the top section or in the base, like the pattern given here.

Maple "Great" chairs probably were brought to Pennsylvania in the extensive German migrations about 1720–1730. This style chair was sometimes called "Grandfather's" and "Grandmother's". Note the delicacy of the front legs compared with the heavy back, seat, and rear posts. The arms and seat are reminiscent of the Wainscot-type chair.

The serviceable three-back slat or ladder-back chair has simple finials and a rush seat. Weaving chair seats with rush and splint was a popular method of seat construction as far back as the seventeenth century when it was used for the Brewster- and Carver-type Pilgrim chairs.

The footstool was used with chairs and settles to keep the feet of the early settlers off the cold floor. Of course, children used them for seats and they were often placed close to the fireplace for warmth. This five-board footstool is similar in construction to the early six-board chest, without the bottom.

A Colonial family would have been very fortunate to have so many mirrors and books in their home as provided here. The early pier mirror and strap sconces, above the half-round table, graced the front hall and parlor area. Books are stored in the wall bookcases of the parlor and hired girl's room.

The stool table or "joint" table between the "Great" chairs served as both chair and table. These stools were also a common item in houses of the late seventeenth century. The legs are pine turnings without any sharp flanges that might be broken off. The four stretchers between the splayed legs served to hold the table together but also, again, to keep feet off the cold floor. The family Bible is lying on the table. (Look for the same Bible in Grandfather's portrait in the blue bedroom.)

There are many variations of the candle stand still in existence today. The candle stand here is a Colonial version of the earliest type of stand which illustrates a medieval pattern of the "cross" base on a tapered column.

The long proportions of the pipe box were necessitated by the long stems of the church-warden clay pipes that were smoked in the 1700s. The little drawer below was filled with tobacco.

CHIPPENDALE WING CHAIR

1. Make a lightweight cardboard pattern of the back (including wings) and the seat. Shirt cardboard or typing paper package inserts are suitable.

2. Place pattern of back on the wrong side of double fabric and trace around the edges.

3. Cut 1/2″ from the pattern line drawn on the fabric.

4. Sew directly on the line marked on the fabric, starting at one side of the bottom and sewing around the back (and wings) to the other side of bottom. There should be an opening across the bottom.

5. Trim seam to 1/4″ and clip into edge to stitching line around curves. (Be careful not to cut stitching.) Do not trim bottom.

6. Turn right side out and slip cardboard pattern into the bottom opening. Keep the seam allowance on *one* side of the cardboard.

7. Stitch dotted lines (shown on the pattern) starting from the top of chair *through* the cardboard and the fabric.

8. Stuff polyester fill from the bottom into the pockets on the side of the cardboard that has the seam allowance. This side is stuffed so that the outside of the chair will be smooth. Stuff firmly around the tops with very little stuffing at the bottom.

9. Sew across the bottom at the cardboard edge and then turn up and stitch the seam allowance to the inside (stuffed side).

10. Place the seat pattern on wrong side of a single piece of fabric and trace around the edge.

11. Cut 1/2″ from the pattern line drawn on the fabric.

12. Place small amount of the polyester fill between the cardboard seat and the wrong side of the fabric. Spread evenly with not much fill at the front section (dotted line).

13. Fold the edges of fabric around the cardboard pattern and sew back and forth across the bottom to secure.

14. Place small end of seat against the stuffed side of the back. Sew to the back from the underside of the chair seat. Bend at dotted line.

15. Bend the wings to the front along the stitched lines. Use a ruler or straight-edge to bend.

16. Sew the front of the chair sides to the side edges of the seat. Sew with tiny stitches up from the bottom and back down from the top, catching both sides of fabric.

17. Turn upside down and squirt glue around the edges of the seat. Allow to dry in this position.

18. Glue the bottom piece made of wood or heavy cardboard to the bottom.

19. Carve legs out of square wood and glue to the bottom.

SLANT-TOP DESK ON FRAME

1. Carve legs as illustrated on pattern using either a 1/4″ dowel or 1/4″ square wood.

2. Glue the lower frame first. Glue end stretchers and ends between legs where indicated on pattern. Allow to dry thoroughly.

3. Glue back piece, middle stretcher, and front drawer rest between leg units, where indicated on pattern. Make sure front drawer rest will allow 7/16″ space for drawer front.

4. Glue lower frame to desk bottom. Legs are set in 1/16″ from the front and sides (flush in back).

5. Glue 2 ends of the other two drawer rests and butt against the back edge of the front drawer rest (in a flat position) and to the lower edge of the back piece.

6. Construct drawer.

7. Glue desk sides to desk back. Hold in upright position until glue sets.

8. Glue front desk panel between desk sides.

9. Glue desk unit to desk bottom.

10. Glue inside shelf 3/8″ below top of back.

11. Glue dividers to shelf, evenly spaced.

12. Glue top of desk to sides and back.

13. Glue strip 2 3/4″ × 1/16″ × 1/16″ on slant top for a paper stop, where indicated on pattern.

14. Hinge slant top to top board.

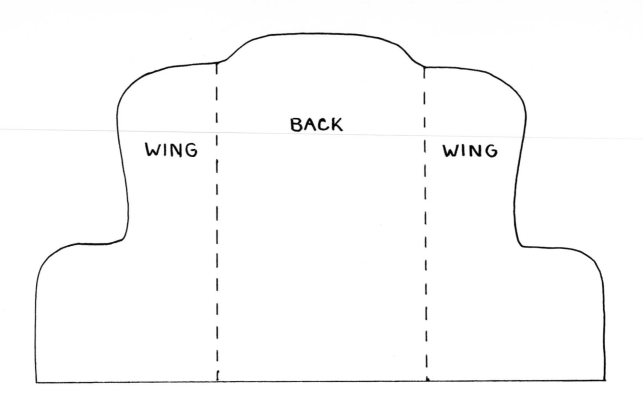

WING   BACK   WING

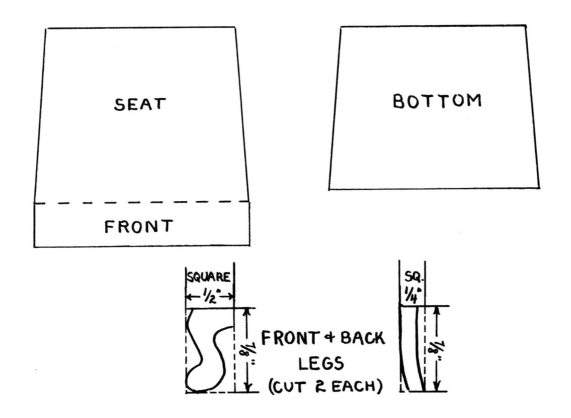

SEAT

FRONT

BOTTOM

SQUARE 1/2"

7/8"

FRONT + BACK
LEGS
(CUT 2 EACH)

SQ. 1/4"

7/8"

CHIPPENDALE WING CHAIR
(CARDBOARD WITH WOOD LEGS)

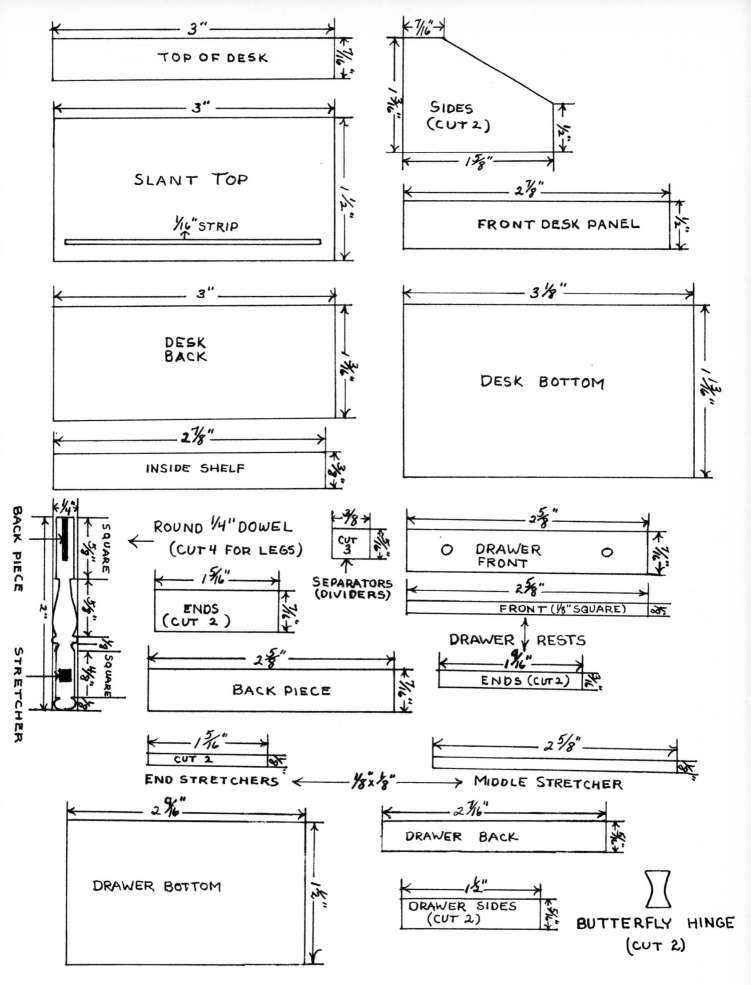

SLANT-TOP DESK ON FRAME — 1/16" BALSA

"GREAT" CHAIRS

1. Glue top back and lower back between the long back slats (2 3/8") in a flat position.

2. Glue four short back slats in a vertical position between the top back and the lower back.

3. Glue the back legs to the edge of seat (1 7/8" edge), lined up to match the long back slats.

4. Carve front legs out of 3/16" square wood as illustrated on the pattern (or use jeweler's files to make the indentations).

5. Sand with an emery board or emery cloth wrapped around a toothpick (for the curved indentations).

6. Glue the front legs to the other 1 7/8" edge of the seat. The back legs will be splayed a bit and the front legs will be straight.

7. Carve, sand, and glue the rungs between the two front legs and between the two side legs. (None in back.) Place the rungs at the upper 5/16" section of the legs.

8. Glue the stretchers below the carved rungs at the lower 5/16" section of the legs. (None in front.)

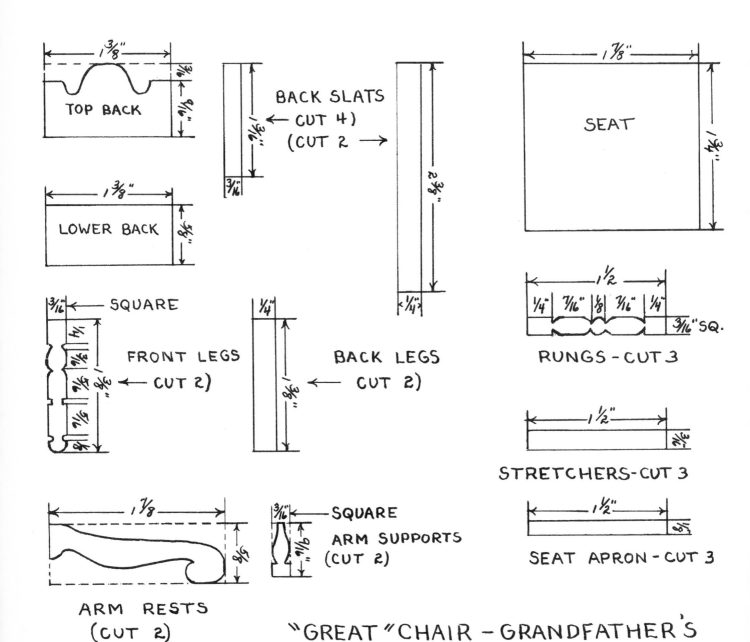

"GREAT" CHAIR – GRANDFATHER'S
1/8" BALSA

70

9. Glue the seat apron pieces between the legs and against the underside of the seat.

10. Glue the back unit to the back edge of the seat. Hold at a slightly reclining angle until the glue sets.

11. Measure and mark arm supports and arm rests for proper placement on the long back slats and the chair seat.

12. Glue the arm supports to the chair seat.

13. Glue the arm rests to the back slats and the arm supports.

14.. A 1/16" strip of balsa is glued around the front and sides to cover the crack between the seat and seat apron pieces.
(Eliminate steps 11, 12, and 13, for Grandmother's "Great" chair.)

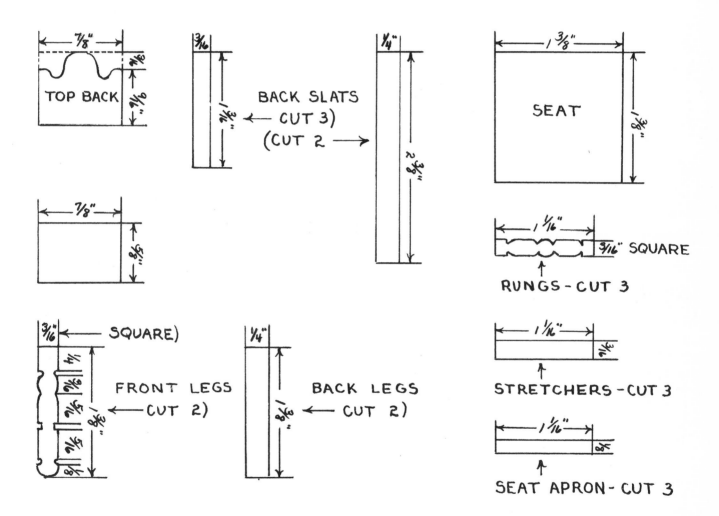

"GREAT" CHAIR — GRANDMOTHER'S
⅛" BALSA

LADDER-BACK CHAIR WITH RUSH SEAT

1. Carve rounded finials on tops of back posts.

2. Glue 1″ slats, 1″ seat rung, and 1″ lower back rung between the back posts where indicated.

3. Sand tops of the front posts until rounded.

4. Glue 1 1/8″ seat rung and 1 1/8″ front rung between the front posts where indicated.

5. Allow both front and back units to dry *thoroughly*.

6. Glue 1 1/8″ seat rungs and 1 1/8″ lower side rungs between front and back units where indicated.

7. See child's high chair in parlor for rush seat directions.

FOOTSTOOL OR BENCH

1. Glue the end edges of the braces and place between the side pieces, set in 1/16″ from the front and back and flush at top.

2. Glue the top edges of the braces and side pieces and place the top board. The top board may be slightly beveled if desired.

3. For a fireside bench make the top board (2 1/2″) and braces (2″) longer.

STOOL TABLE

1. Carve the legs from 1/4″ dowel or square piece of wood.

2. Finish the rough shape of legs by sanding with an emery board or emery cloth.

3. Score drawer front with a dull pencil on one of the short apron pieces or construct a real drawer.

4. Glue the apron pieces between the top of the legs. Legs will angle out because of the shaved ends of the apron pieces.

5. Glue the ends of the stretcher pieces and place between the legs in the middle of the lower squared section of the legs.

6. The edges of the top board should be slightly beveled with a sand paper block or emery board.

7. Glue the top of legs and apron pieces and place the top board.

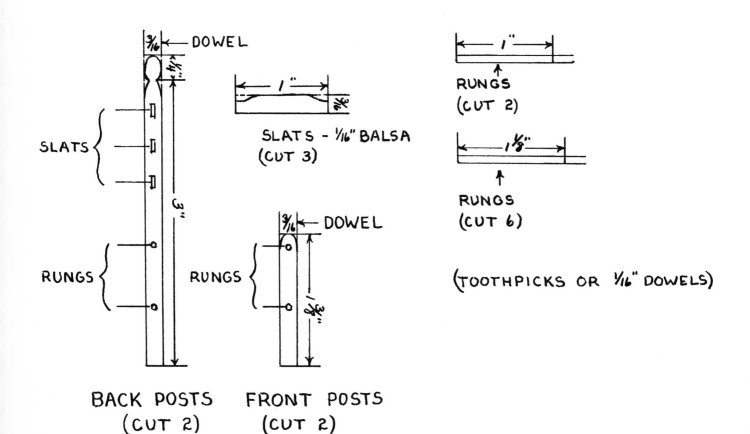

BACK POSTS (CUT 2)   FRONT POSTS (CUT 2)

SLATS - 1/16″ BALSA (CUT 3)

RUNGS (CUT 2)

RUNGS (CUT 6)

(TOOTHPICKS OR 1/16″ DOWELS)

SLATS

RUNGS   RUNGS

LADDER-BACK CHAIR (RUSH SEAT)

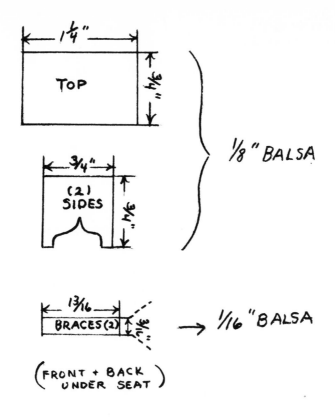

1¼"

TOP

3/8"

} ⅛" BALSA

3/4"

(2)
SIDES

3/8"

13/16"

BRACES (2)

1/8"

→ 1/16" BALSA

(FRONT + BACK
UNDER SEAT)

FOOT STOOL OR BENCH - ⅛" + 1/16"

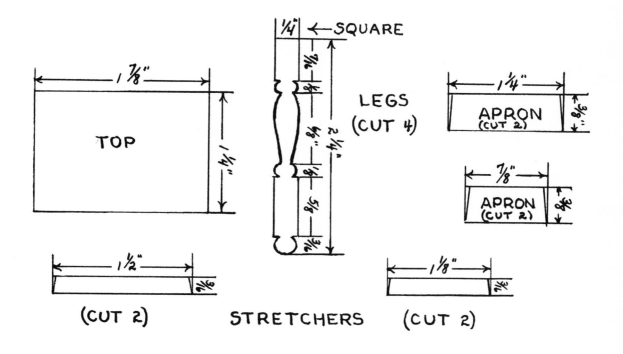

¼" ← SQUARE

9/32"

⅛"

4/8"

⅛"

5/8"

3/32"

LEGS
(CUT 4)

2¼"

1⅞"

TOP

1¼"

1½"

3/32"

(CUT 2)

STRETCHERS

1⅛"

3/32"

(CUT 2)

1¼"

APRON
(CUT 2)

3/8"

⅞"

APRON
(CUT 2)

3/8"

STOOL TABLE - ⅛" BALSA

CANDLE STAND

1. Taper stem using a sandpaper block.

2. Glue brace across the grain on the underside of top.

3. Glue and pin top to small end of stem.

4. Shape foot. Cut indentations into each piece as shown in the sideview illustration.

5. Glue the foot pieces together to form a cross.

6. Glue and pin the foot to the bottom of the stem.

HALF-ROUND TABLE

1. Taper the legs on a sandpaper block.

2. Glue two legs at the rear corners of top and two legs at the front as indicated.

3. Glue the apron pieces across front and sides of the round edge of table top between legs as indicated.

4. Sand the top rail so that it is rounded (three-cornered) and glue to the back edge of table top. (Rounded section facing front and the back flush.)

WALL BOOKCASE

1. Cut side pieces as shown on pattern.

2. Glue shelves between sides where indicated.

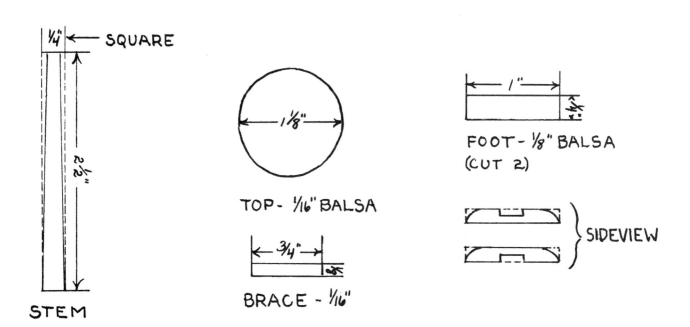

STEM

TOP- 1/16" BALSA

BRACE - 1/16"

FOOT- 1/8" BALSA (CUT 2)

SIDEVIEW

CANDLE STAND

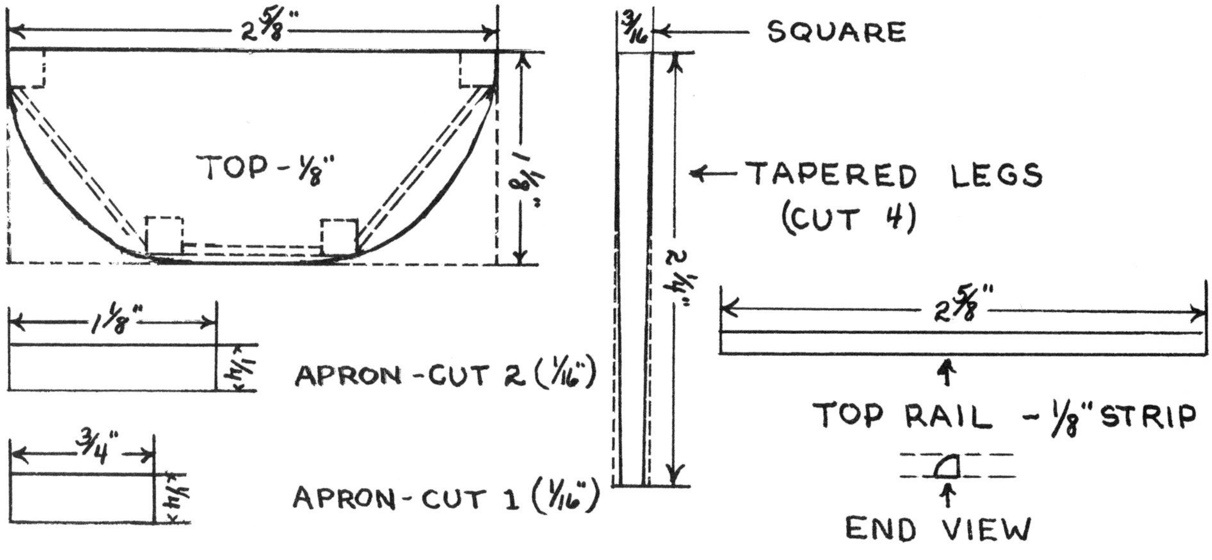
2 5/8"
TOP - 1/8"
1 1/8"
3/16
SQUARE
TAPERED LEGS
(CUT 4)
2 1/4"
2 5/8"
1 1/8"
1/4"
APRON - CUT 2 (1/16")
3/4"
1/4"
APRON - CUT 1 (1/16")
TOP RAIL - 1/8" STRIP
END VIEW

HALF - ROUND TABLE

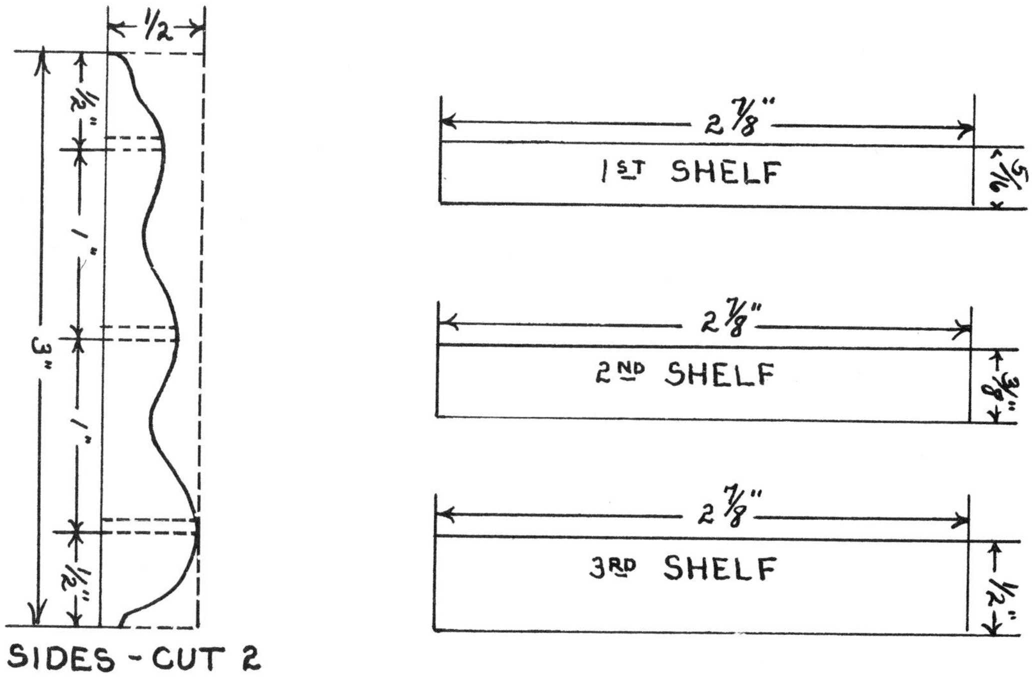
1/2
1/2"
1"
3"
1"
1/2"
SIDES - CUT 2
2 7/8"
1ST SHELF
5/16
2 7/8"
2ND SHELF
3/8"
2 7/8"
3RD SHELF
1/2"

WALL BOOKCASE - 1/16" BALSA

BACK HALL

The back entrance of a Colonial New England town house was used by members of the family and tradespeople. It was customary to hang a lantern just inside the door, ready to be taken off its peg to be used to light the entrance and garden area. The diamond panes of the whaler's lantern hung here on the wall next to the steps are typical of the seventeenth-century American casement window. This type of lantern was probably used on an American whaling ship, hence its name. The candle is inserted by opening the little door in front.

Just below the lantern is a peg rack for hanging outdoor garments, as well as the cane and "French" umbrella shown in the picture. (It is surprising that the umbrella or "canopy" dates back to the 1700s.)

The turned post at the foot of the stairs is made of pine and has no flanges that project far enough out to risk getting knocked off in that vulnerable spot. Pine turnings had the disadvantage of not holding up well where subjected to much wear. Pine tops, backs, frames, and drawer parts were used more extensively than pine turnings for this reason. Many early pieces were made by using a combination of hard and soft woods, depending upon the function of the furniture. Tables often had pine tops with hardwood legs.

WHALER LANTERN

1. Cut diamond shape holes out of back, front, and sides.

2. Score door lines with pencil on front piece.

3. Glue toothpick slice on door front for nob.

4. Glue "Sculpey" (or toothpick) candle to center of bottom piece.

5. Glue side pieces *between* front and back.

6. Glue bottom in place.

7. Glue top to lantern unit.

8. Glue leather or fabric strap handle to sides above diamonds.

PEG COAT RACK

1. Shape ends of pegs.

2. Glue pegs on pegboard pattern.

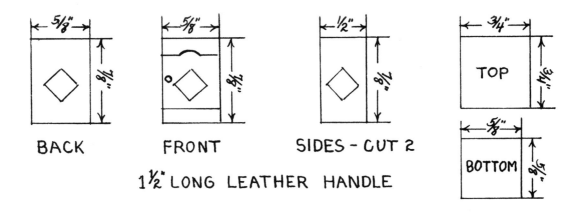

BACK   FRONT   SIDES - CUT 2

1½" LONG LEATHER HANDLE

WHALER LANTERN - 1/16"

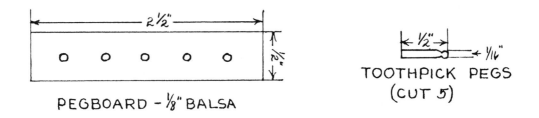

PEGBOARD - 1/8" BALSA

TOOTHPICK PEGS
(CUT 5)

PEG COAT RACK

BLUE BEDROOM

The "blue" bedroom is decorated to enhance the blue English delft tiles around the face of the fireplace. These tiles are paper miniatures that can be purchased at dollhouse-supply shops. Grandfather's stern portrait, which shows the family Bible, hangs above the mantle.

The "deed" box containing the family's valuable papers is on the blanket chest. (Every dollhouse should have a deed box.) Little boxes similar to this were made for a wide variety of purposes. Some rested on a chest or table and held the family Bible, jewelry, or other valuables. Many small boxes were fashioned to hang on the wall and were used to hold spices, salt, candles, etc. They were convenient for storage and, best of all, were out of the reach of mice.

Chests were common during the Colonial period and were used for traveling, storage, tables, chairs, and even as beds for small children. As the chest evolved, drawers were added below the well—first one, as here, and later more and more until the well was eliminated entirely and the "highboy" came into being. A beaded-edged mirror hangs above the blanket chest.

The slender, graceful columns of the maple "pencil post" bed support a canopy of glazed-wool hangings that match the wallpaper. The bed steps were necessary to reach the bed, which was usually some distance from the floor in order to avoid drafts. If you want to be very authentic, the mattress can rest on top of ropes (carpet thread) stretched back and forth across the bed and around pegs which are attached to the frame.

Fringe finishes off the curtains and matching homespun bedspread. The bed hangings and curtains are tied back with navy blue ball-fringe.

A curved-back wing chair, upholstered in blue plaid, is placed adjacent to the fireplace. The ratchet candle stand next to the chair can be raised or lowered for reading by adjusting the ratchets.

The blanket rack or stand doubled for drying clothes during the long winter months when it was too cold to hang them outdoors.

DEED BOX

1. Cut drawer front from front piece or score drawer front with a pencil.

2. Glue shelf to front and back pieces where indicated on pattern. Hold in place until glue sets.

3. Glue ends between front, back, and shelf.

4. Glue box unit to center of base.

5. Construct drawer if you have not simulated one by scoring.

6. Glue dowel or toothpick slices to front for pulls.

7. Attach the top lid to box with hinges.

8. Bevel the edges of the box base by careful sanding with an emery board.

9. Trim around base of box unit with 1/16" strips.

BLANKET CHEST

1. Cut drawer front out of front piece.

2. Glue inside shelf and bottom between sides.

3. Glue front and back against shelf, bottom, and sides, with tops flush. Front and back are set *between* sides.

4. Construct drawer.

5. Cut 1/4" dowel slices and glue to drawer front for drawer pulls.

6. Glue 1/16" × 1/8" × 1 3/4" strips on each end of the underside of lid.

7. Bevel top edges of lid and round strips on underside of lid (at ends).

8. Center the lid on top and attach with hinges.

9. Glue 1/16" strip across bottom front.

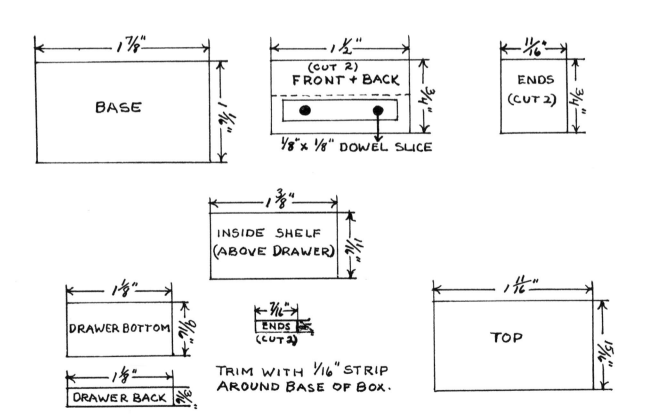

DEED BOX - 1/16" BALSA

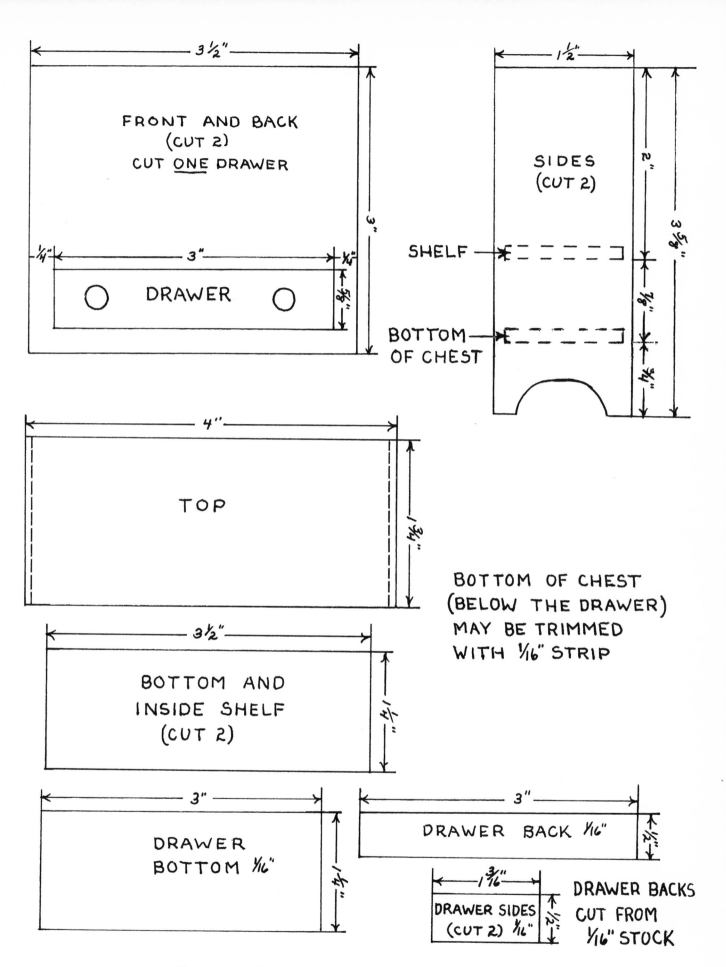

FRONT AND BACK
(CUT 2)
CUT ONE DRAWER

3½"

3"

¼" 3" ¼"

DRAWER

⅝"

SIDES
(CUT 2)

1½"

2"

3⅝"

SHELF

⅞"

BOTTOM
OF CHEST

¾"

TOP

4"

1¾"

BOTTOM OF CHEST
(BELOW THE DRAWER)
MAY BE TRIMMED
WITH 1/16" STRIP

BOTTOM AND
INSIDE SHELF
(CUT 2)

3½"

1¼"

DRAWER
BOTTOM 1/16"

3"

1¼"

DRAWER BACK 1/16"

3"

½"

DRAWER SIDES
(CUT 2) 1/16"

1 3/16"

½"

DRAWER BACKS
CUT FROM
1/16" STOCK

BLANKET CHEST — 1/8" + 1/16"

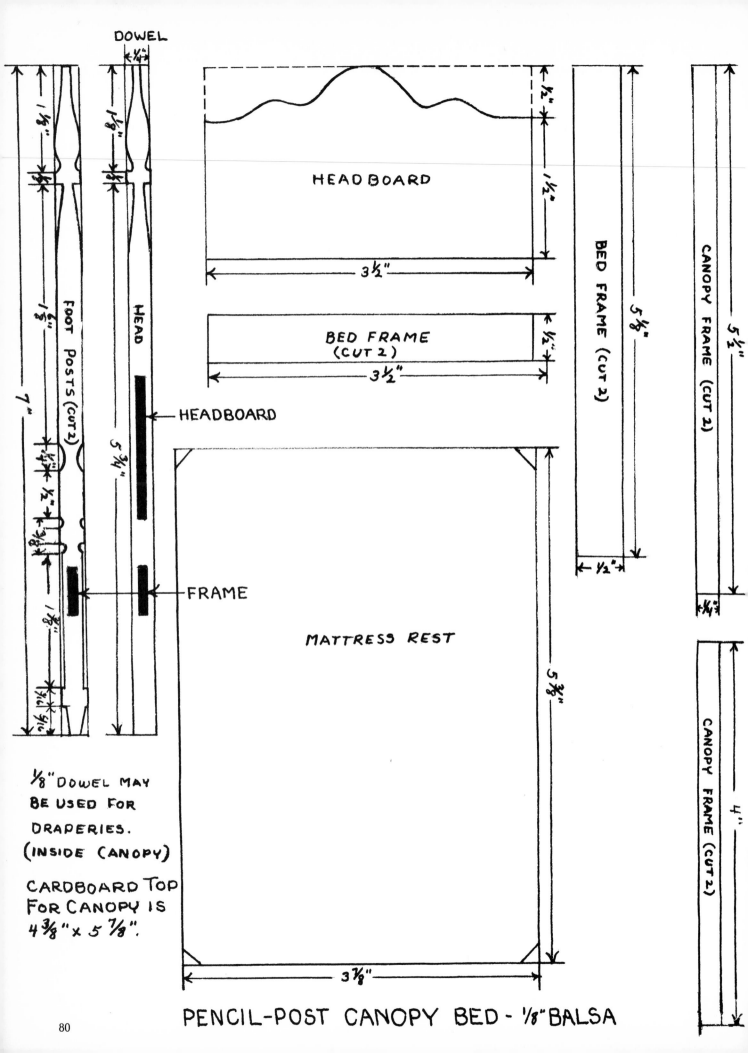

DOWEL

$\frac{1}{4}"$

$1\frac{1}{2}"$

$\frac{1}{8}"$

$\frac{3}{4}"$

HEAD BOARD

$\frac{1}{2}"$

$1\frac{1}{2}"$

$3\frac{1}{2}"$

BED FRAME (CUT 2)

$5\frac{7}{8}"$

CANOPY FRAME (CUT 2)

$5\frac{1}{2}"$

$1\frac{5}{8}"$

$7"$

FOOT POSTS (CUT 2)

HEAD

HEADBOARD

BED FRAME
(CUT 2)

$\frac{1}{2}"$

$3\frac{1}{2}"$

$5\frac{3}{4}"$

$1\frac{1}{4}"$

$\frac{1}{2}"$

$\frac{3}{16}"$

$1\frac{3}{8}"$

FRAME

$\frac{9}{16}"$

$\frac{1}{2}"$

MATTRESS REST

$5\frac{7}{8}"$

CANOPY FRAME (CUT 2)

$\frac{1}{4}"$

$4"$

CANOPY FRAME
(CUT 2)

$\frac{1}{8}"$ DOWEL MAY
BE USED FOR
DRAPERIES.
(INSIDE CANOPY)

CARDBOARD TOP
FOR CANOPY IS
$4\frac{3}{8}" \times 5\frac{7}{8}"$.

$3\frac{7}{8}"$

PENCIL-POST CANOPY BED - $\frac{1}{8}"$ BALSA

PENCIL-POST CANOPY BED

1. Carve posts as illustrated on the pattern, using either a 1/4″ pine dowel or 1/4″ piece of square wood. If pine dowels are used, the lower portion of the foot posts may be squared for a better butt joint but this is not necessary.

2. Glue the headboard and one of the short (3 1/2″) bed frame pieces between the head posts.

3. Glue the other short bed frame piece between the foot posts. Allow the headboard and foot units to dry thoroughly.

4. Glue the long bed frame pieces between the head and foot units.

5. Cut off the corners of the mattress rest.

6. Glue mattress rest in place between the four posts on top of the frame.

7. Glue the long pieces of the canopy frame (5 1/2″) to the top of the posts in a flat position.

8. Glue the short pieces of the canopy frame (4″) against the ends of the long pieces in a side position.

9. Cover the cardboard top (tester) and add a ruffle (not more than 1″ wide) around the sides.

10. Glue the covered tester to the canopy frame.

11. Hem side and head-end draperies and slide onto 1/8″ dowel pieces (previously measured to fit between the posts).

12. Glue dowels (with draperies) in place between the posts.

BED STEPS
1. Cut hole in back.

2. Glue steps between sides where indicated.

3. Glue back to sides and top step.

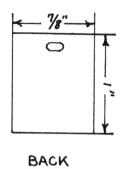

BACK

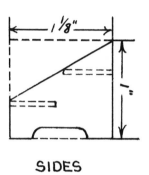

SIDES

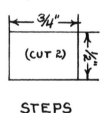

STEPS

BED STEPS - 1/16"

UPHOLSTERED BEDROOM CHAIR

1. Make a lightweight cardboard pattern of the back (including wings) and the seat. Shirt cardboard or typing-paper package inserts are good.

2. Place the pattern of the back on the wrong side of fabric and trace around the edges. Cut two.

3. Cut the fabric 1/2" from the pattern line drawn on the fabric.

4. Sew directly on the line marked on the fabric, starting at one side of the bottom and sewing around the back (and wings) to the other side of bottom. There should be an opening across the bottom.

5. Trim seam to 1/4" and clip into the edge to the stitching line around curves. Be careful not to cut stitching. Do not trim bottom.

6. Turn right side out and slip cardboard pattern into the bottom opening. Keep the seam allowance on *one* side of the cardboard.

7. Stitch on dotted lines (shown on the pattern), starting from the top of the chair *through* the cardboard and the fabric.

8. Stuff polyester fill from the bottom into the pockets on the side of the cardboard that has the seam allowance. This side is stuffed so that the outside of the chair will be smooth. Stuff firmly around the tops with very little stuffing at the bottom. Encourage the cardboard to curve into a rounded back. Not much stuffing will go into the upper wings.

9. Sew across the bottom at the cardboard edge and then turn up and stitch the seam allowance to the inside (stuffed side).

10. Place the seat pattern on wrong side of a single piece of fabric and trace around the edge.

11. Cut 1/2" from the pattern line drawn on the fabric.

12. Place a small amount of the polyester fill between the cardboard and the wrong side of the fabric with not much fill at the front section.

13. Fold the edges of the fabric around the pattern and sew back and forth across the bottom to secure.

14. Place small end of the seat against the stuffed side of the back. Sew to the back from the underside of the chair seat. Bend at dotted line.

15. Sew the front of the chair sides to the side edges of the seat.

16. Turn upside down and glue around the edges of the seat. Allow to dry in this position.

17. Cut the bottom piece out of wood or heavy cardboard and glue to bottom.

18. Cut fabric 24" × 1" for the flounce. Turn under and press 1/4" hem on both long sides. Ruffle or pleat one edge.

19. Glue the ruffle to the bottom of chair. Narrow rick-rack may be glued over the upper hem stitching.

RATCHET CANDLE STAND

1. Glue uprights to bottom with exactly 5/8" space in between.

2. Glue ratchet to exact center of ratchet rest.

3. Slide ratchet-rest into position along edges of uprights.

4. Fasten ratchet-stop to upright with pin. Cut off shank of pin in rear, allowing enough to bend over to secure.

5. Slide crosspiece (with hole) over end of ratchet and glue into place on top of the uprights.

6. Glue top sides to top (long sides between short sides) around edges to form 1/16" lip. Bottoms will be flush.

7. Glue top to ratchet.

8. Glue braces in a flat position on each side of ratchet and against underside of top.

BLANKET RACK

1. Sand top of uprights until rounded.

2. Glue bars to uprights.

3. Sand the feet at ends until rounded as illustrated in sideview on pattern sheet.

4. Glue uprights to feet.

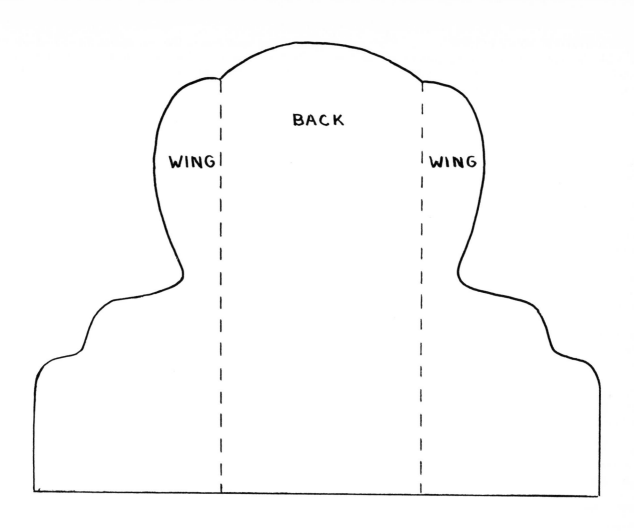

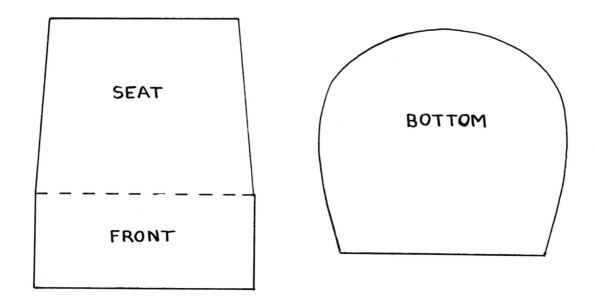

UPHOLSTERED BEDROOM CHAIR
(CARDBOARD)

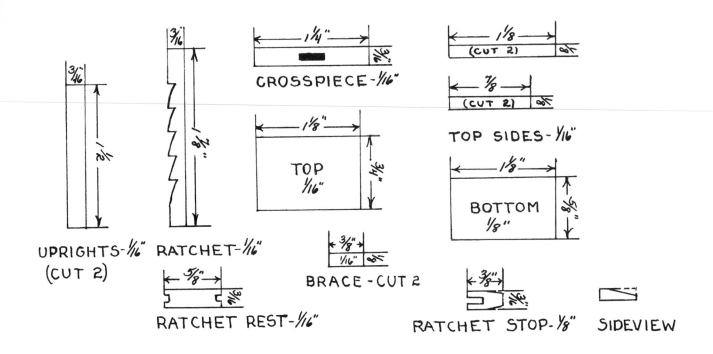

UPRIGHTS-1/16" (CUT 2) RATCHET-1/16"

CROSSPIECE-1/16"

TOP 1/16"

BOTTOM 1/8"

TOP SIDES-1/16" (CUT 2)

BRACE-CUT 2

RATCHET REST-1/16"

RATCHET STOP-1/8" SIDEVIEW

RATCHET CANDLE STAND

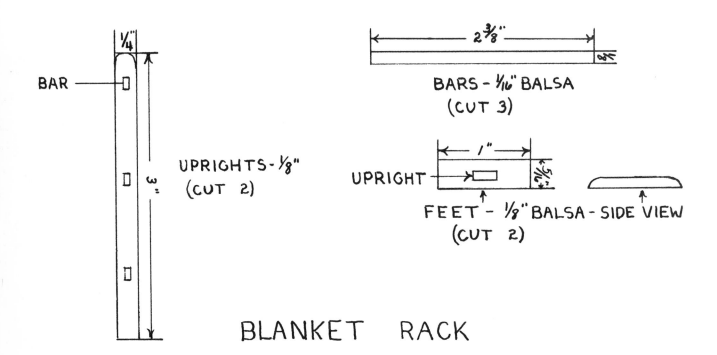

BAR

UPRIGHTS-1/8" (CUT 2)

BARS-1/16" BALSA (CUT 3)

UPRIGHT

FEET-1/8" BALSA-SIDE VIEW (CUT 2)

BLANKET RACK

RED BEDROOM

The sturdy ball-and-bell four-poster bed is a perennial favorite. If you look just below the ball top, you will discover the bell shape, which is repeated again in the next turning.

Quite different from the other candle stands is the pine bedside table. The tapered legs give it a delicate appearance. This style lamp-table, or stand, is also in wide use today, attesting to the fact that Colonial furniture was truly well-designed and utilitarian.

The child's settle is constructed in much the same manner as the large settle located in the weaving room. The hole in the back is for lifting it from place to place. The little chair is currently occupied by a doll.

The hooded cradle originated in Vermont. Of course, the purpose of the hood was to protect the child from drafts. The rockers are designed so that the cradle can not be tipped too far and up-end "baby and all."

Beautifully-shaped arms highlight the five-back, or ladder-back rocker. The center sections are curved, with thickened ends to assure a solid foundation for the pinning or joining process. The sled-type rockers are pinned into the slotted ends of the posts.

The Pennsylvania Dutch dower chest is my favorite piece. (Its full-size twin can be found in the State museum in Harrisburg, Pennsylvania). The Pennsylvania Dutch loved to decorate their furniture with cheerful, happy colors. The heart, bird, and tulip designs are found on many old pieces. My daughter's initials and the date I made the chest are painted in the center of the heart.

Grandmother's portrait hangs above the mantle in this bedroom. Both Grandfather and Grandmother are portrayed wearing rather Puritan-looking attire, probably their "go-to-meeting" clothes.

BALL-AND-BELL FOUR-POSTER BED

1. Carve posts from 3/8" pine dowel or a 3/8" piece of square wood. If pine dowels are used, the lower portion of the posts may be squared off to provide a better butt joint with the bed frame.

2. Finish the rough shape of the posts by sanding with emery boards or emery cloth wrapped around a circular shape the same size as the indentation (toothpick or thin pencil).

3. Taper the ends of the headboard by shaving or sanding the 1/8" thickness of the wood to 1/16".

4. Glue the headboard and one of the short bed frame pieces (3 1/2") between the head posts where marked on the pattern.

5. Glue the other short bed-frame piece to the foot posts where marked on the pattern. Allow to dry thoroughly.

6. Glue the long (5 1/2") bed-frame pieces to the head and foot units.

7. Cut the corners out of the mattress rest and glue on top of the bed frame between the four posts.

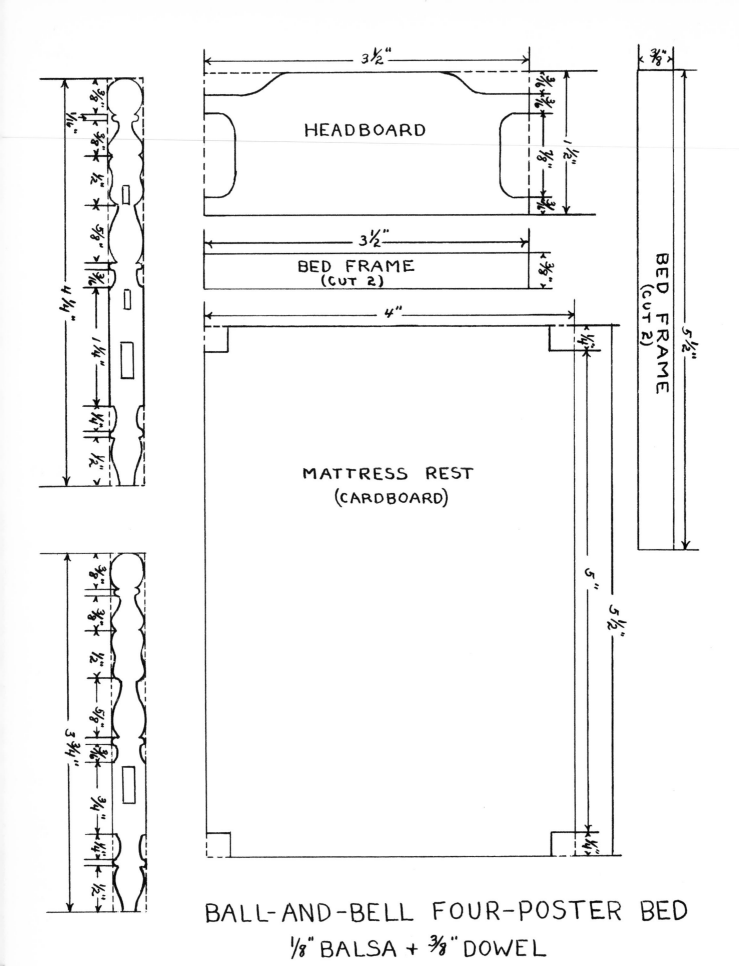

HEADBOARD

3½"

3/16" + 3/8"

1½"

3/8"

3/16"

BED FRAME
(CUT 2)

3½"

3/8"

MATTRESS REST
(CARDBOARD)

4"

¼"

5"

5½"

¼"

BED FRAME
(CUT 2)

3/8"

5½"

3/8"

4¼"

3/16"

1¼"

¼"

½"

5/8"

½"

3/16"

3/8"

3¾"

3/16"

3/4"

¼"

½"

5/8"

½"

3/8"

3/8"

BALL-AND-BELL FOUR-POSTER BED
⅛" BALSA + ⅜" DOWEL

CANDLE STAND

1. Taper the legs with a knife from a 1/4" square strip of wood. Shave gradually to the end on all sides so that the legs will be four-sided (not round), or sand until tapered using a sandpaper wood block.

2. Sand the legs lightly with a sandpaper block or an emery board.

3. Score drawer front with a dull pencil in one of the apron pieces.

4. Glue the apron pieces between the top of the legs.

5. The edges of the top board should be slightly beveled with an emery board.

6. Glue the top of legs and the tops of the apron pieces and center the top board.

CHILD'S SETTLE

1. Glue ends to back piece, having back piece extend 1/4" above the top of end pieces (1/4" from floor).

2. Glue three edges of the seat and place against back and end pieces 5/16" from floor, as indicated on the pattern.

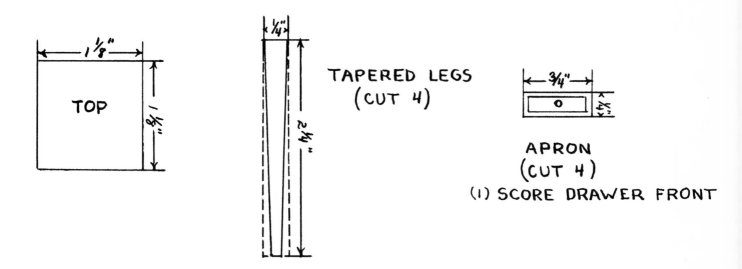

CANDLE STAND - ⅛" BALSA

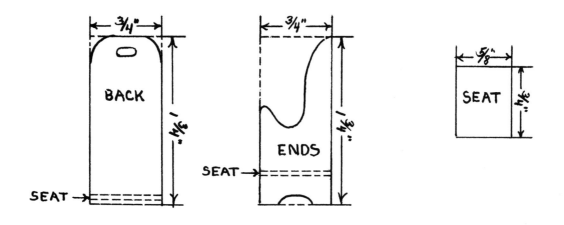

CHILD'S SETTLE
¹⁄₁₆" BALSA

VERMONT HOODED CRADLE

1. The bottom piece is slightly larger than side measurement to allow angle of back and foot pieces. Bevel ends of bottom slightly, as indicated on side pattern.

2. Glue back to bottom at slight angle to match angle of side pieces. Do not allow glue to set permanently before step 3 is completed.

3. Glue side pieces to back and bottom edges. Hold until glue sets.

4. Glue foot to bottom and side pieces.

5. Glue front hood in place, matching straight forward edge of sides.

6. Glue top center and then top sides to form roof of hood.

7. Glue rockers to bottom where indicated on bottom pattern.

8. Paint interior of cradle a compatible opaque color.

LADDER-BACK ROCKER WITH RUSH SEAT

1. Carve rounded finials on tops of back posts.

2. Cut or saw indentations into bottom of posts for rocker insertion, as illustrated on the front posts pattern piece. (Be sure the cut is from front to back when gluing slats and rungs.) Do all four posts.

3. Glue 1″ slats, 1″ seat rung, and 1″ lower back rung between the back posts where indicated on the pattern sheet. The cut at the bottom of the post should be running in the opposite direction to the glued slats and rungs.

4. Shape the tops of front posts.

5. Glue 1 1/8″ seat rung and 1 1/8″ front rung between the front posts. Again, the cut at the bottom of the posts should be running in the opposite direction to the glued rungs.

6. Allow both front and back unit to dry *thoroughly*.

7. Glue 1 1/8″ seat rungs and 1 1/8″ lower side rungs between front and back units where indicated.

8. Carve "mushroom" arms as shown on the pattern piece. Refer to the sideview illustration.

9. Glue arms on top of front posts and against back posts (level with the second ladder from the bottom).

10. Shape rockers as illustrated.

11. Glue chair to rockers at high points of rockers. The rockers are inserted into the cuts at the bottom of chair posts.

12. See child's high chair in keeping room for rush seat directions.

PENNSYLVANIA DUTCH DOWER CHEST

1. Glue upper sides between upper front and back.

2. Glue upper unit to one of the bottom pieces so that there is a 1/8″ extension on the front and sides; back will be flush.

3. Glue lower sides between lower front and back.

4. Glue lower unit to the other bottom piece with the same 1/8″ extension.

5. Glue the upper and lower units together, back flush.

6. Glue the drawer-divider in the exact center between the upper and lower bottoms.

7. Glue the front and back leg pieces to the lower bottom, flush with edges of lower bottom.

8. Glue the side legs to the lower bottom between the front and back leg pieces.

9. Score the drawer fronts with a dull pencil to create a paneled effect, or bevel from the front to back edges by careful sanding, using a wood block.

10. Construct drawer. The drawer sides and back rest on the bottom, the front butted against it.

11. Hinge top.

12. Paint the chest an apple green.

13. Transfer the designs to the chest.

14. Paint the bird blue, the tulips and heart scallops yellow, the cherries and heart red, and the leaves and vines dark green. Initials and date may be painted inside heart.

15. Antique with a dark green glaze.

16. Varnish or spray finish.

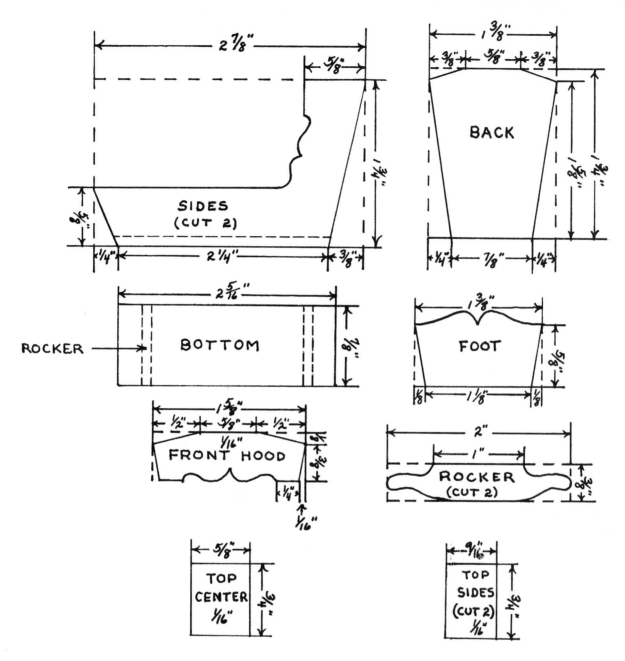

(TOP PIECES AND FRONT HOOD CUT FROM 1/16" STOCK.)

VERMONT HOODED CRADLE

1/8" BALSA

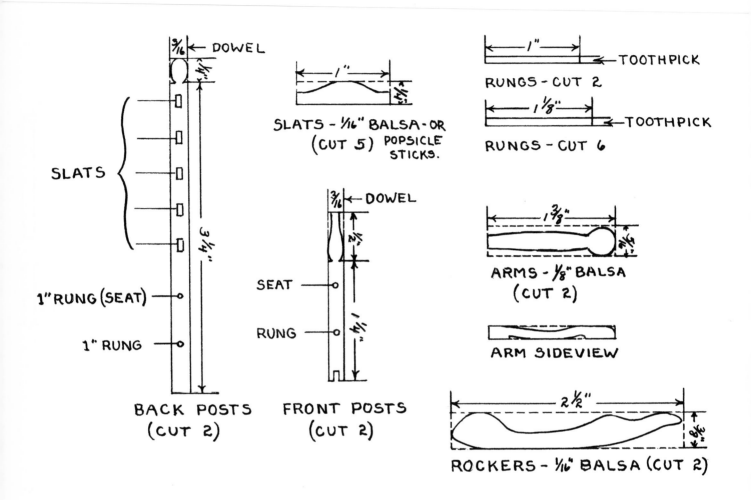

DOWEL

3/16"
1/4"

SLATS

3/4"

1" RUNG (SEAT)

1" RUNG

BACK POSTS
(CUT 2)

SLATS - 1/16" BALSA - OR
(CUT 5) POPSICLE
STICKS.

1"

DOWEL

3/16"
1/2"

SEAT

RUNG

1 3/4"

FRONT POSTS
(CUT 2)

1"
TOOTHPICK
RUNGS - CUT 2

1 1/8"
TOOTHPICK
RUNGS - CUT 6

1 3/8"
3/16"
ARMS - 1/8" BALSA
(CUT 2)

ARM SIDEVIEW

2 1/2"
3/8"
ROCKERS - 1/16" BALSA (CUT 2)

LADDER-BACK ROCKER WITH RUSH SEAT

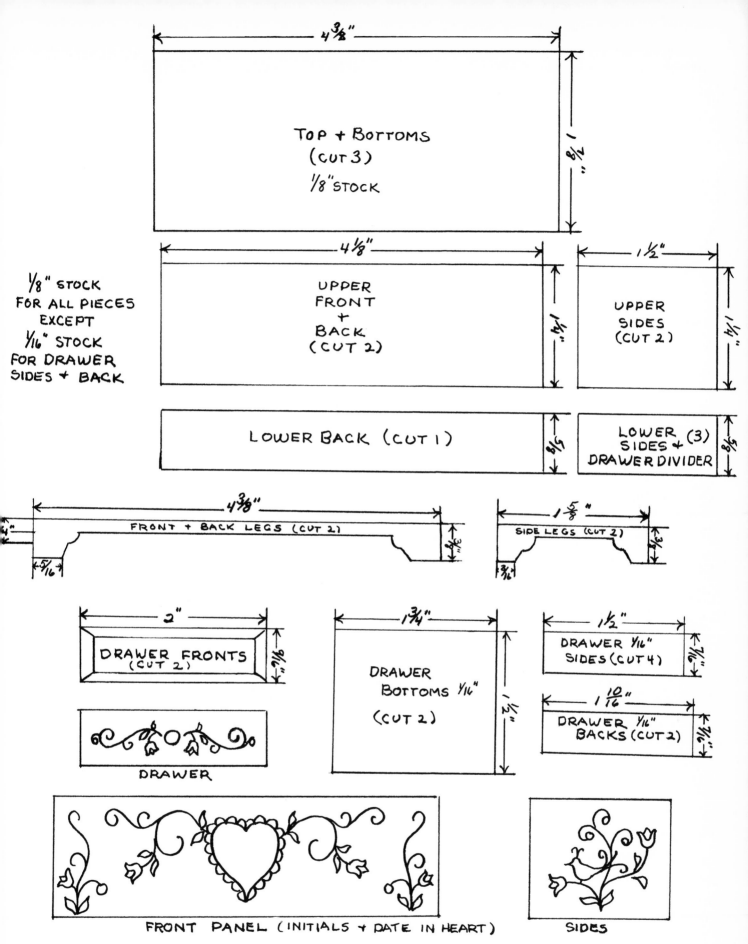

TOP + BOTTOMS
(CUT 3)
1/8" STOCK

4 3/8"

8 1/2"

1/8" STOCK
FOR ALL PIECES
EXCEPT
1/16" STOCK
FOR DRAWER
SIDES + BACK

UPPER
FRONT
+
BACK
(CUT 2)

4 1/8"

1 1/4"

UPPER
SIDES
(CUT 2)

1 1/2"

1 1/4"

LOWER BACK (CUT 1)

5/8"

LOWER (3)
SIDES +
DRAWER DIVIDER

5/8"

FRONT + BACK LEGS (CUT 2)

4 3/8"

3/4"

5/16"

SIDE LEGS (CUT 2)

1 5/8"

3/4"

3/16"

DRAWER FRONTS
(CUT 2)

2"

9/16"

DRAWER

DRAWER
BOTTOMS 1/16"
(CUT 2)

1 3/4"

1 1/2"

DRAWER 1/16"
SIDES (CUT 4)

1 1/2"

7/16"

DRAWER 1/16"
BACKS (CUT 2)

1 10/16"

7/16"

FRONT PANEL (INITIALS + DATE IN HEART)

SIDES

PENNSYLVANIA DUTCH DOWER CHEST

(HEART, BIRD + TULIP)
1/8" BALSA

BATH

The "bath" area is not a bathroom in the present day sense. This small area is furnished with a washstand which closets the family chamber pot. A water pitcher and bowl, plus soap and towels, enable our Yankee family to subscribe to the old adage that "Cleanliness is next to Godliness."

Early cupboards ranged from open shelves or "side boards" to the hutch, which was originally just a storage area with a door or lid. (Illustrated by the hutch table in the keeping room.) This armoire, or wardrobe, falls into the latter category. Wardrobes (clothes presses) were with or without drawers and shelves. The enclosed section on the upper shelf of some cupboards is called an ambry and originally was a storage area for firearms. The wardrobe here sits on a carved base and has a mitered crown rising above the top board—rather a massive piece, similar to the Dutch "kas."

WASHSTAND

1. Score drawer on top front. Insert a round-headed pin in center of drawer or glue a toothpick slice to the drawer for drawer pull. Clip shank in rear.

2. Glue top sides between top front and back.

3. Glue top unit to center shelf, positioned to the rear so that the back is flush and the front and sides of board extend slightly.

4. Cut hole (1 1/4" × 7/8") in lower front for the door.

5. Glue 1/16" thickness of wood for the trim on a 1/16" thick door measured to fit the hole. Use a pin or dowel slice as before for the door pull.

6. Fasten the door to the front piece with hinges on the right hand side of the opening. Hinges should be glued to the back of the door and to the back of the front piece so that they won't show. A heavy grade of typing paper makes a satisfactory hinge.

7. Glue one edge of the bottom-side pieces and place on the bottom back to form a right angle. Hold in position until the glue sets.

8. Glue end edges and one long edge of the bottom shelf and place between the sides and against the back just above legs.

9. Glue the forward edge of the bottom shelf and the forward edge of the side pieces and place the front piece.

10. Glue the top unit to the bottom unit, keeping the back flush.

11. Bevel the edges of the top with a sanding block or an emery board and fasten to the top unit with hinges at each end. Keep back flush.

12. Glue ends of bar (trimmed toothpick) between the towel-rack ends and then glue to the side of washstand.

ARMOIRE

1. Glue one long edge of side pieces and place on each end of the back piece to form a right angle. Hold in place until the glue sets.

2. Glue end edges and one long edge of the bottom shelf and place between the sides and against the back at the bottom of unit.

3. Glue the top board facing across the front at the top of the unit.

4. Glue the top facing and top sides together, placing the side pieces between the front and back. The top will angle outward.

5. Glue the top in place on the angled top pieces and then glue to the unit.

6. Glue bottom sides between bottom front and back (the widest leg on the bottom side pieces toward the rear).

7. Glue the bottom unit to armoire.

8. Glue 1/16" thick trim to the doors. Place a heavy book on the doors until they are dry to prevent warping.

9. Attach door to side pieces with hinges about 1" × 3/4".

10. Insert a pin with a round head through the door where marked on pattern and clip excess shank in the rear. Put a drop of glue on the back where the pin is cut off. Alternatively, you can use a toothpick slice glued to the door for a pull.

11. Glue a small dowel to the side pieces inside the armoire for hanging clothes.

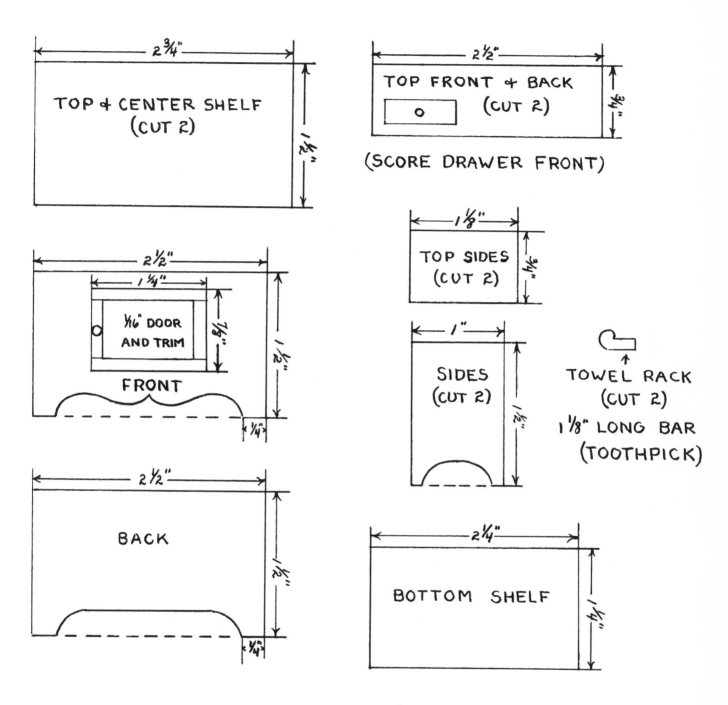

TOP & CENTER SHELF
(CUT 2)
2¾"
1½"

TOP FRONT & BACK
(CUT 2)
2½"
¾"
(SCORE DRAWER FRONT)

TOP SIDES
(CUT 2)
1⅛"
¾"

FRONT
2½"
1¼"
⅟₁₆" DOOR AND TRIM
⅞"
1½"
¼"

SIDES
(CUT 2)
1"
1½"

TOWEL RACK
(CUT 2)
1⅛" LONG BAR
(TOOTHPICK)

BACK
2½"
1½"
¼"

BOTTOM SHELF
2¼"
1¼"

WASHSTAND - ⅛" BALSA

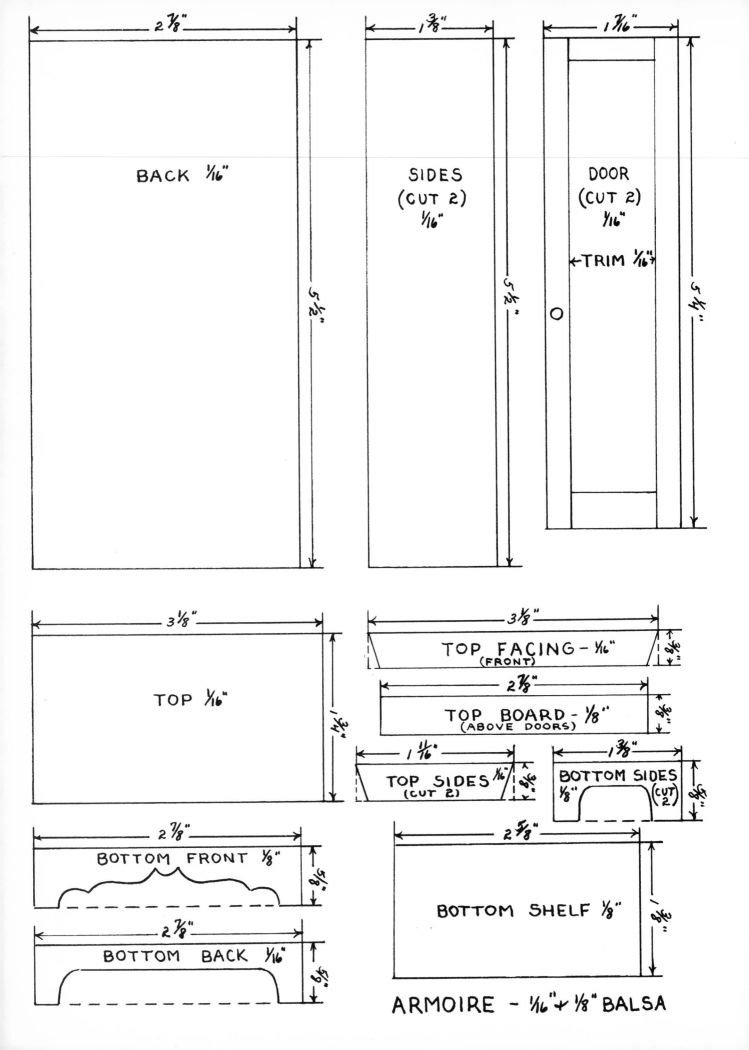

BACK 1/16"

2 7/8"

5 1/2"

SIDES
(CUT 2)
1/16"

1 3/8"

5 1/2"

DOOR
(CUT 2)
1/16"

←TRIM 1/16"

1 7/16"

5 1/4"

TOP 1/16"

3 1/8"

1 3/4"

TOP FACING - 1/16"
(FRONT)

3 1/8"

3/8"

TOP BOARD - 1/8"
(ABOVE DOORS)

2 7/8"

3/8"

TOP SIDES
(CUT 2)
1/16"

1 1/16"

3/8"

BOTTOM SIDES
1/8"
(CUT 2)

1 3/8"

3/8"

BOTTOM FRONT 1/8"

2 7/8"

5/8"

BOTTOM BACK 1/16"

2 7/8"

5/8"

BOTTOM SHELF 1/8"

2 5/8"

1 3/8"

ARMOIRE - 1/16" + 1/8" BALSA

WEAVING ROOM

I became fascinated with the art of weaving when I began to research the spinning wheel. *Foxfire I*, a wonderful book, furnished a description of the entire process. This spinning wheel is as authentic as I could make it. Unfortunately, it still won't spin a thread. However, the wheel will turn and move the cord (carpet thread) around the spindle.

The yarn winder *does* actually work. Its purpose is simply to wind the thread into skeins to be used for knitting or weaving. Note the knitting on the settle and the skeins in the bowl, a "found" object.

The loom is stored in pieces behind the settle. I would like to attempt a working miniature loom for the Colonial Doll House at some future date.

Fireside seats, or settles, provided a warm draft-free place for Colonial families to sit and pursue quiet activities. These seats were constructed with high, sometimes curved, backs. Some had a shelf to hold a lamp or candle for reading. Our settle has an armrest to hold a hot drink or a candle. A little box (like the candle box) is attached to the back for books, or whatever. Quite often the seat area provided storage for bedding and sometimes the seat was entirely separate from the back and could be converted into a bed by tilting the seat forward to form a box.

A three-legged stool, such as the one in the weaving room, could have been found almost anywhere in a Colonial setting—from the barn (milking stool) to the parlor.

The six-board chest is a basic box-type construction. This chest, with leather strap hinges, is used for the storage of woolens. I fancy that the hired girl was very adept at weaving and spent many hours at work in the weaving room.

SPINNING WHEEL

1. The wheel rim can be made by gently bending dampened mat board or bass wood into a circular shape. It measures 10 3/16" (plus a hair fraction) long, 1/8" wide, and 1/16" thick. Score a groove into the center of the wheel rim (before bending) for the cord to run in as the wheel turns. Glue ends together.

2. Carve eight round toothpicks for the spokes.

3. Carve the wheel hub out of a pine dowel.

4. Place the wheel hub in the center of the wheel (lay flat on a piece of wax paper) and glue the spokes to the hub and wheel. Use snap clothespins to hold spokes in place until glue dries.

5. Taper spindle end of platform piece, which should be a 3/16" thick piece of pine to provide sufficient weight for the wheel. Balsa wood for this piece may be too light.

6. Shape the wheel post and spindle posts.

7. Shape toothpicks for the spindle assembly and glue (in holes) to 1/8" dowel piece which is then glued to the spindle post. (A 1/16" hole is drilled into the dowel to attach to the spindle post.)

8. Shape the peg to connect the spindle posts.

9. Drill 1/16" holes through the spindle posts for the peg.

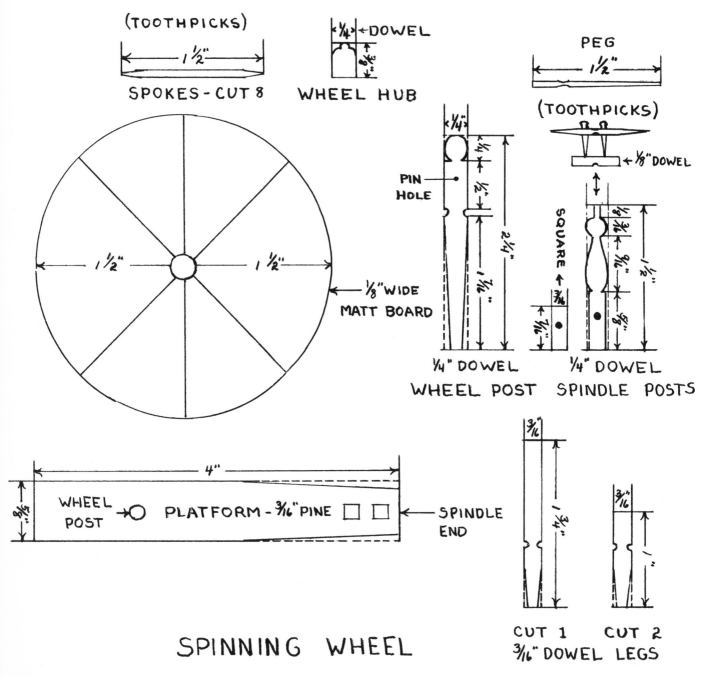

(TOOTHPICKS)
1½"
SPOKES - CUT 8

¼" →DOWEL
WHEEL HUB

PEG
1½"
(TOOTHPICKS)
←⅛" DOWEL

PIN HOLE
⅛" WIDE MATT BOARD

¼" DOWEL
WHEEL POST

SQUARE
¼" DOWEL
SPINDLE POSTS

1½"
1½"

WHEEL POST PLATFORM - 3/16" PINE ☐ ☐ ← SPINDLE END
4"

3/16"
CUT 1   CUT 2
3/16" DOWEL LEGS

SPINNING WHEEL

10. Drill a small hole through the wheel post (large enough for a sequin pin to pass through freely). Drive the point of the pin (after passing through the wheel post) into the large end of the wheel hub. The wheel should now turn on the pin.

11. Sand the bottoms of the spindle posts and the wheel post at a slight angle. Glue the posts onto the platform piece, at an outward angle.

12. Shape the legs as illustrated and again sand the bottoms at a slight angle.

13. Glue the two short legs at the wheel end (splayed outward for good balance) and the long leg at the spindle end, set in about 1/2" from ends.

14. Fasten heavy carpet thread around the wheel and connect to the spindle. Tie and glue knot.

YARN WINDER

1. Glue six lengths of 1/16" dowel to ends of spokes (see spoke end illustration in pattern). Use snap clothespins to hold spokes in place until glue dries.

2. Glue spokes of wheel around 3/8" dowel hub, where indicated on the pattern sheet.

3. Bevel ends of legs so they will be splayed slightly for better balance.

4. Glue legs to underside corners of base, set in 1/16".

5. Glue sides to back piece at one end.

6. Glue front to sides.

7. Glue top and bottom in place to form a box on top of the back piece.

8. Glue finial to top of box.

9. Drill hole, slightly larger than a sequin pin, through center of wheel hub.

10. Insert pin through wheel hub and into top front of box (check to make sure wheel will clear base when attached).

11. A small round piece of wood may be glued to pin head to cover it.

12. Glue back (wheel unit) to base.

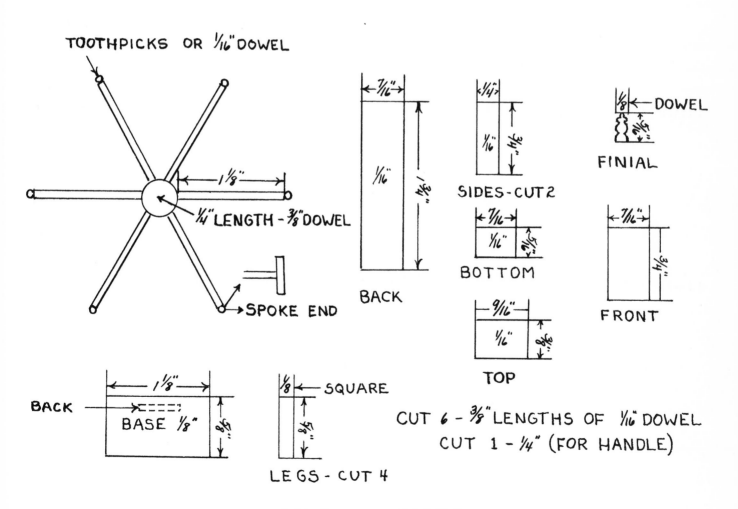

YARN WINDER

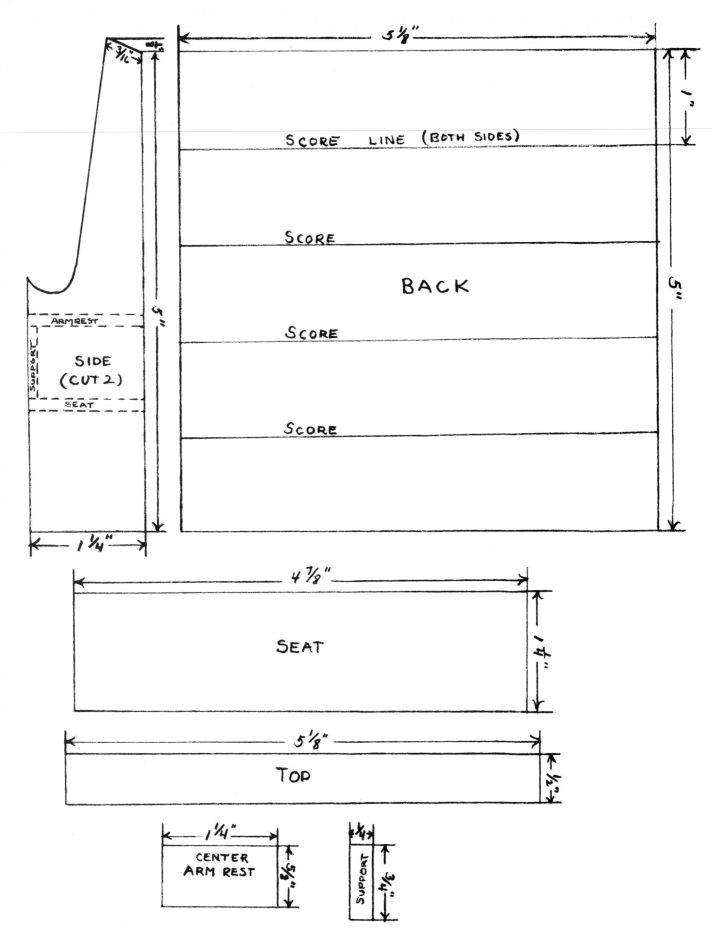

SETTLE - ⅛" BALSA

SETTLE

1. Score back or glue individual boards together. Score on both sides using a dull pencil.

2. Glue side pieces to back at each end. Hold in upright position until glue sets.

3. Glue seat to sides and back where indicated on pattern.

4. Glue the upright support to armrest, at center front.

5. Glue armrest to back of settle and the upright support to the seat, centered on the bench.

6. Glue top to sides and back.

7. Bevel top board on the front and back by sanding with a wood block.

8. A receptacle similar to the candle box may be glued to the back above the arm rest. (See pages 111 and 112 for candle box directions.)

STOOL

1. Bevel edges of top.

2. Round bottoms of legs.

3. Bevel tops of legs slightly so that they will splay outward.

4. Glue legs to underside of top.

SIX-BOARD CHEST

1. Glue bottom to ends where indicated on pattern.

2. Glue front and back boards to end edges, with tops even.

3. Attach top with thin leather, fabric or paper hinges.

4. Bevel the lid on the front and sides. The front will extend to make it easy to open.

5. A 1/16" strip may be glued above the feet, around the sides and front of the chest for trim.

6. Many of these chests were decorated with "scratching" (scoring with a sharp instrument to create a design). They were also hand-painted with various decorations.

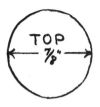

TOP
7/8"

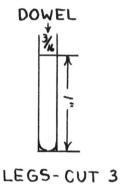

DOWEL
3/16

LEGS- CUT 3

STOOL - 1/8" BALSA

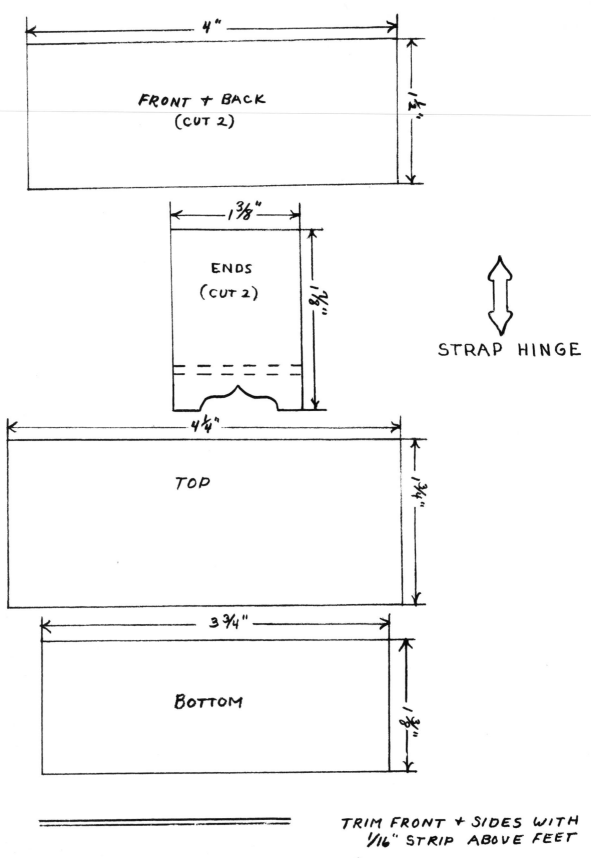

4"

FRONT + BACK
(CUT 2)

1½"

1⅜"

ENDS
(CUT 2)

1⅞"

STRAP HINGE

4¼"

TOP

1¾"

3¾"

BOTTOM

⅞"

TRIM FRONT + SIDES WITH
1/16" STRIP ABOVE FEET

(USE LEATHER STRAP HINGES)

SIX BOARD CHEST - ⅛" BALSA

HIRED GIRL'S ROOM

In Colonial days you would not expect the hired girl's room to be so well-furnished. However, if she were a relative and considered part of the family, she certainly would be well-provided for, even to the extent of having a few books in her bookcase, as well as her own Bible (lying on the blanket chest). In addition to a simple desk-bench for writing, the blanket chest, and the hired man's bed (so called because the low posts make it practical to use under the eaves), there are washing and grooming articles, a mirror over the mantle, and the inevitable chamber pot.

The desk bench is an unusual piece that would have been made by some talented joiner for a special order. It reminds one of later-style school desks.

Ball feet, used here on the blanket chest, were often found on Colonial pieces. A later version was the "ball and claw" foot. These feet added a decorative touch and provided a sturdy base for chests and other pieces.

The hired-man's bed has a dust ruffle since it is used here for a young lady. The mattress, or straw, was placed in the box-like frame, rather than on top of ropes or boards.

The courting mirror, sometimes called the hired-man's mirror, is, in this case, a little larger scale than is authentic. These small mirrors, usually quite plain, were often found in Colonial homes and, it is said, were used by younger members of the family to primp a bit in preparation for courting.

DESK-BENCH

1. Glue back onto the seat at right angles. Hold until glue sets.

2. Glue ends to back and seat, keeping top of back and top of ends even.

3. Glue braces under the seat and against the end pieces.

4. Glue desk rest to left end piece where indicated on the pattern.

5. Glue the desk board to top of desk rest.

BALL-FEET BLANKET CHEST

1. Glue back to bottom at right angles. Hold in place until glue sets.

2. Glue end-pieces to back and bottom.

3. Glue one long edge and both end-edges of shelf and place between ends and against back where indicated on the pattern.

4. Glue front piece against bottom and ends, keeping tops flush and leaving the opening at the bottom for the drawer.

5. Construct drawer.

6. Carve feet out of 3/8" dowel.

7. Glue the feet to bottom corners.

8. Glue dowel slices (1/8") to drawer front for pulls.

9. Glue 1/8" strips to the underside edges of the top to form a lip to hold the top in place. No hinges are necessary.

10. Bevel the top edges.

11. Glue 1/8" strips around the front and ends of bottom. Bevel edges.

HIRED MAN'S BED

1. Carve posts using either a 3/8" dowel or 3/8" square wood.

2. Taper ends of head board to 1/16".

3. Glue one end rail and head board between two posts where indicated on the pattern.

4. Glue the other end rail between the other two posts. Allow to dry.

5. Glue the side rails between the head and foot units of bed, where indicated on pattern.

6. Cut the corners from the mattress-rest. Mattress-rest may be made from cardboard, mat board, or wood.

7. Glue the mattress-rest to the *bottom* edges of rails to form a recessed area for the mattress.

WALL BOOKCASE

1. Glue shelves to sides where indicated on pattern, with the first, narrow shelf at the top, the third shelf flush with the side pieces at the bottom.

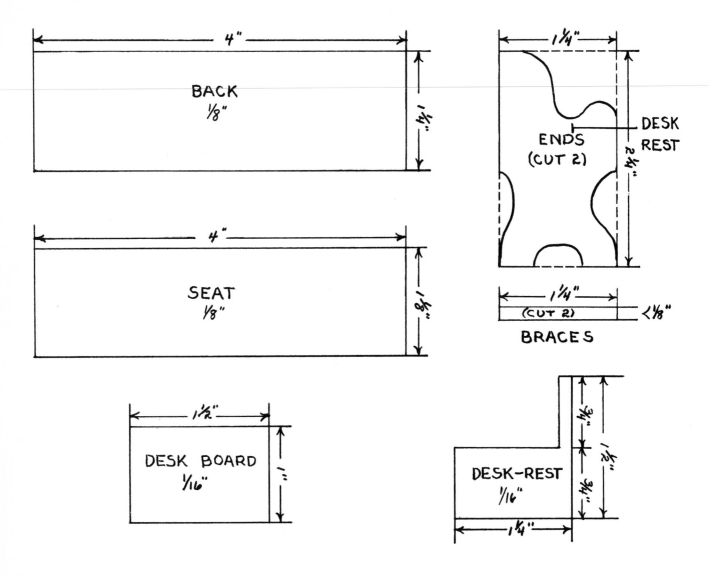

BACK
⅛"

4"

1¼"

SEAT
⅛"

4"

1⅛"

ENDS
(CUT 2)

1¼"

2¼"

DESK REST

1¼"
(CUT 2)
<⅛"

BRACES

DESK BOARD
1/16"

1½"

1"

DESK-REST
1/16"

¾"

½"

¾"

1¼"

DESK--BENCH

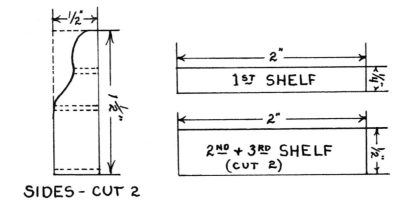

SIDES - CUT 2

½"

1½"

1ˢᵀ SHELF

2"

¼"

2ᴺᴰ + 3ᴿᴰ SHELF
(CUT 2)

2"

½"

WALL BOOKCASE -- 1/16"

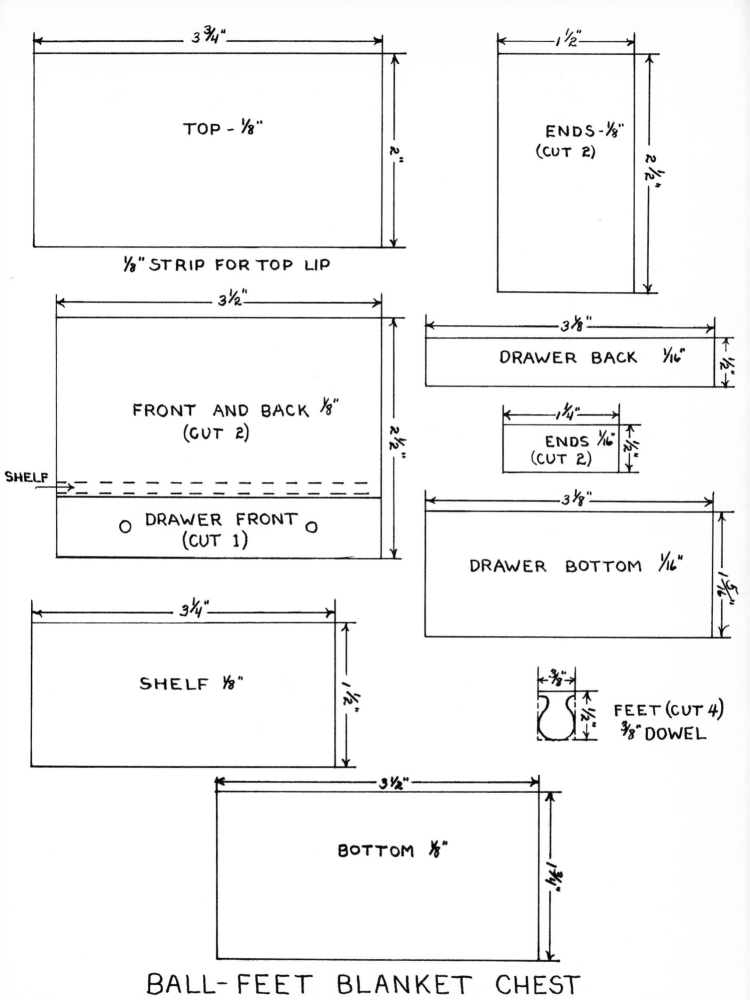

TOP - ⅛"

⅛" STRIP FOR TOP LIP

ENDS - ⅛"
(CUT 2)

DRAWER BACK 1/16"

ENDS 1/16"
(CUT 2)

FRONT AND BACK ⅛"
(CUT 2)

SHELF

DRAWER FRONT
(CUT 1)

DRAWER BOTTOM 1/16"

SHELF ⅛"

FEET (CUT 4)
⅜" DOWEL

BOTTOM ⅛"

BALL-FEET BLANKET CHEST

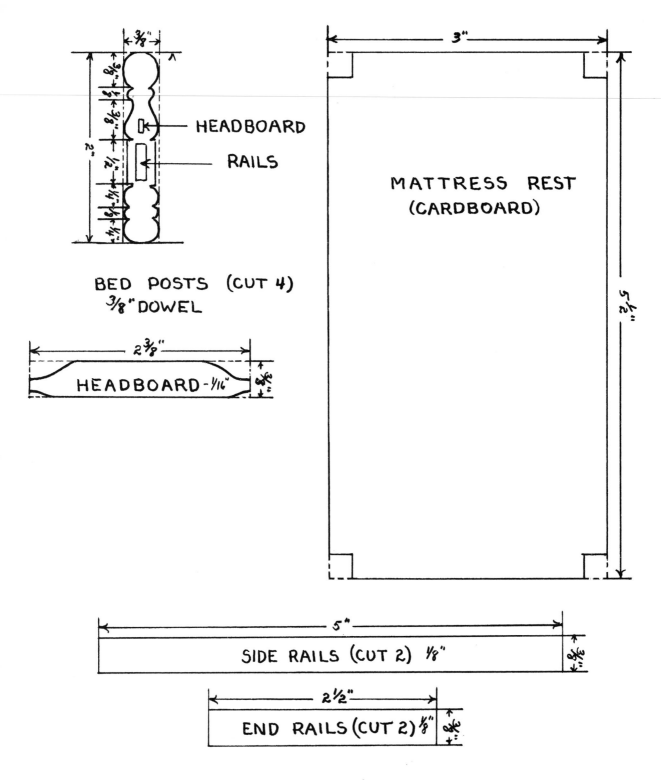

BED POSTS (CUT 4)
3/8" DOWEL

HEADBOARD

RAILS

HEADBOARD - 1/16"

MATTRESS REST
(CARDBOARD)

SIDE RAILS (CUT 2) 1/8"

END RAILS (CUT 2) 1/8"

HIRED MAN'S BED

Accessories

Once your Colonial dollhouse is furnished, you will want to fill it with accessories typical of 1776 homes—cooking utensils, dishes, food, cleaning items, fireplace equipment, linens, books, pictures, mirrors, and other personal effects—to make the house a real home. I used tin, wood, cardboard, leather, and Sculpey for most accessories; fabrics for curtains and linens; and yarn for rugs.

Metal items are really quite easy to make. Thin tin, aluminum, brass, and copper sheets can be purchased at hobby shops, if you prefer to invest in these materials, but I have found household tin cans easy to work. Some cans have a copper or brassy-colored lining and some even have a pewter-like finish on the inside (good for steins, dinner plates, etc.). I also used TV dinner plates, as well as tin cans, for many items that need small parts, such as candle holders. The griddle is made from a lightweight bottle screw cap. Many implements found in early Colonial homes were made of black wrought iron, which can be simulated by painting the tin, wire, or Sculpey a flat black. Incidentally, a drop of liquid soap added to paint will help it to stick to tin and other slick surfaces.

You will need the following materials to make the tin items:

Lightweight tin cans (evaporated milk cans are good)
Lightweight metal screw cap
Wire cutter and thin wire
Contact tube cement or clear-drying epoxy glue
Tin cutter (pedicure scissors work well for small pieces)
1/8" size tin "curler" (found in hobby shops)
Awl or thumbtack
Pliers with flat nose, smooth-jaws (for bending and crimping tin)
Tweezers
Flat black paint

From the keeping room: broom; painted tray; water bench with funnel, beer stein, water dipper, and oaken buckets; slipper rocker; hutch table with candle mold and clay fruit bowl; wood box, flatware tray and kitty.

The smaller wood accessories, such as frames, painted tray, etc. are made from balsa wood. The butter churn, "oaken" buckets, and firkins are made from lightweight cardboard for the round areas and balsa wood for the tops and bottoms. A good lightweight cardboard to use would be a cereal box or bun box. Poster board of similar weight and texture is excellent. Cardboard can be bent into a desired shape more easily if it is first dipped quickly into water. These round items can be made by bending wood (see bending wood, page 56), but it is easier to use cardboard, which can be stained or painted to look very much like wood. You will need the same materials and tools for making balsa wood and cardboard accessories as for making furniture from these materials. (See page 54.)

As previously mentioned, Sculpey is a commercial clay that can be purchased at most hobby shops and art supply stores. It is used for dishes, jugs, food, and some of the fireplace equipment, as well as other personal effects found in the Colonial Dollhouse. The clay is fashioned into the desired shape with various home tools, ranging from cuticle orange sticks to marbles (for rounded bottoms). As in the construction of the bricks (see page 31),

the modeled clay is baked in a home over (300 degrees F. for 20 minutes) and painted with acrylic paints to achieve nice bright colors. A little brown may be added to soften or tone down a *too* bright color.

Salt dough, also called baker's dough, and bread dough can also be used to make miniature food items and other accessories. Salt dough makes very realistic pies and bread, baked in a bottle cap (fluted edge), or you can fashion your own tins. Bread dough is air-dried, as are some of the commercial clays found in hobby shops. Candles can be fashioned from any of these malleable materials or made from the ends of round toothpicks.

To make salt dough, combine 1 cup flour, 1/2 cup salt, and 1/2 cup water (or coffee for a light brown color). Knead and leave in the refrigerator overnight. Bake at 325 degrees F. for 40 minutes.

Bread dough is made from 3 slices of stale white bread (remove crusts), 3 tablespoons of white glue, and 3 drops glycerine. Tear bread into small pieces, add glue, and mix with your fingers. Knead until smooth. Water-soluble paint can be mixed with dough until it is the desired color or dough may be painted after it is dry. Store in the refrigerator until you are ready to mold it.

From the parlor: half-round table with tin tray and vase of flowers, foot stool, slant-top desk on frame with tin inkwell, ladder-back chair with rush seat, Chippendale mantle clock, braided rug, and bellows.

TINWARE

SKILLET
1. Bend and glue rim around edge of bottom piece.

2. Bend handle (see pattern) and glue next to rim seam.

3. Paint flat black.

4. Glue to implement board. (See page 119)

STRAINER
1. Punch holes in strainer with awl or thumb tack.

2. Bend handle (see skillet).

3. Paint flat black.

4. Glue to implement board.

SPATULA
1. Bend handle (see skillet).

2. Paint flat black.

3. Glue to implement board.

TONGS
1. Bend two pieces of tin (see pattern).

2. Glue tops together.

3. Paint flat black.

4. Glue to implement board.

SHOVEL
1. Punch hole in handle with awl or thumb tack.

2. Bend handle (see skillet).

3. Sides of shovel may be bent to form scoop.

FLATWARE
1. Bend handles of spoons and forks (see skillet).

2. Store in flatware tray.

FUNNEL
1. Bend into circular funnel shape.

2. Glue seam.

3. A small piece of drinking straw may be glued to tip of cone and painted to match, or a small piece of tin may be used for the spout.

WATER DIPPER
1. Bend sides into circular shape to fit bottom piece.

2. Glue seam.

3. Glue sides to bottom.

4. Bend handle as illustrated on pattern sheet and glue next to seam at the top of cup.

BREAD KNIFE
1. Insert narrow blade end cut from tin into center of wood handle (1/2" × 1/8" × 1/8").

2. Round the wood handle and strain.

FIREPLACE CRANE
1. Paint flat black.

2. Fasten to side of cardboard fireplace with wire.

GRIDDLE
1. Cut griddle base from bottle screw cap (such as a soda bottle cap). Cut down to approximately 1/8" on sides.

2. Punch holes at opposite sides with awl or thumb tack.

3. Cut 3 1/2" piece of wire and insert ends into holes and twist to fasten handle.

BEER STEINS
1. Bend sides into circular shape to fit bottom piece.

2. Glue seam.

3. Glue sides into bottom piece.

4. Bend top into cone shape, closed at tip.

5. Bend handles (A and B) as illustrated on pattern.

6. Glue handle A next to side seam.

7. Glue sharp curve of handle B to top of A with long end of B resting on edge of cup.

8. Glue cone on top with long end of B glued to inside.

CANDLE MOLD
1. Cut corners of top and bottom to dotted line. (Use TV dinner plate foil for top tray.)

2. Turn edges upward along dotted lines with pliers to form lip on trays.

3. Curl six candle forms (from lightweight tin foil) using 1/8" tin curler.

4. Glue candle forms to bottom tin tray, three to a side.

5. Glue top tray (lightweight foil) to top of candle forms with edge turned upward.

6. Shape handle and glue narrow end over edge of top tray and wide end against candle forms.

7. Punch holes carefully with awl through foil on top tray into the candle forms.

CHANDELIER

1. Cut into round base to dotted line.

2. Bend arms upward to dotted circular line on base, forming lip.

3. Bend arms downward and then up again with the last 1/8″ straight (to glue candle base onto).

4. Curl six candle holders with 1/8″ tin-curler.

5. Glue candle holders to candle bases.

6. Glue candle bases to ends of arms.

7. Shape the cone and glue seam with small hole at tip to insert chain.

8. Twist chain length in opposite direction every 1/4″ and bend loop in top for hanging.

9. Glue large end of cone to base (inside lip).

10. Glue chain into top of cone.

CANDLE HOLDER WITH WIND PROTECTOR

1. Bend sides into circular shape to fit base.

2. Glue ends together.

3. Glue sides to base.

4. Curl candle holder with 1/8″ tin curler.

5. Glue candle holder to base.

6. Bend the other 3/4″ piece to form handle.

7. Glue handle to sides as illustrated on pattern sheet.

From the hired girl's room: hired man's bed, ball-feet blanket chest with accessories, desk-bench, braided rug, and chamber pot.

WALL SCONCE

1. Bend base forward along dotted line.

2. Bend sides of base upward and bend edges of reflector forward, using pliers.

3. Curl candle holder with 1/8″ tin curler.

4. Glue candle holder to base.

5. Punch hole in reflector with awl or thumb tack.

CANDLE HOLDER

1. Bend edges of base upward, using pliers.

2. Curl candle holder with 1/8″ tin curler.

3. Glue candle holder to base.

4. Bend handle around dowel for circular shape.

5. Glue handle to base.

FOOD WARMER

1. Bend across middle section on both dotted lines to form top.

2. Bend bottom of legs outward at dotted lines to form feet.

3. Paint flat black.

4. Punch holes in top with awl.

INK WELL

1. Bend sides into circular shape and glue seam.

2. Glue to base. (Pen quill is carved from a flat toothpick.)

TRAY

1. Bend edges of tray upward using pliers.

TINWARE ACCESSORIES

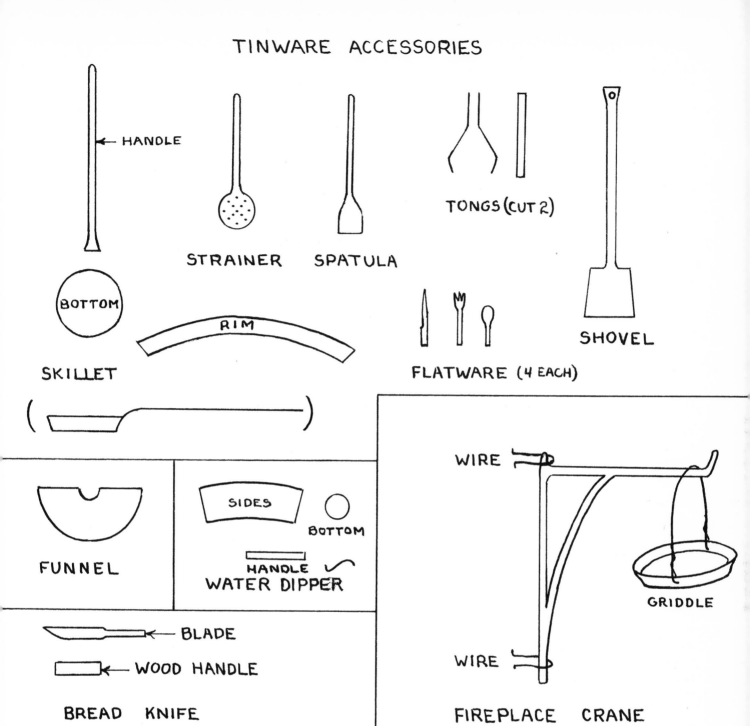

HANDLE

STRAINER   SPATULA   TONGS (CUT 2)   SHOVEL

BOTTOM

SKILLET   RIM   FLATWARE (4 EACH)

FUNNEL

SIDES   BOTTOM

HANDLE

WATER DIPPER

BLADE

WOOD HANDLE

BREAD KNIFE

WIRE

WIRE

GRIDDLE

FIREPLACE CRANE

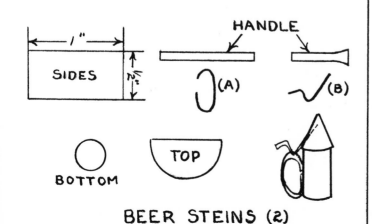

HANDLE

1"

SIDES   2½"   (A)   (B)

BOTTOM   TOP

BEER STEINS (2)

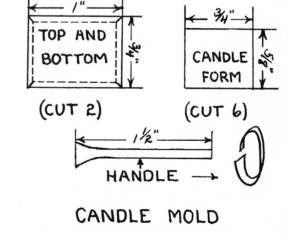

1"

TOP AND BOTTOM   ¾"

(CUT 2)

¾"

CANDLE FORM   ⅝"

(CUT 6)

1½"

HANDLE

CANDLE MOLD

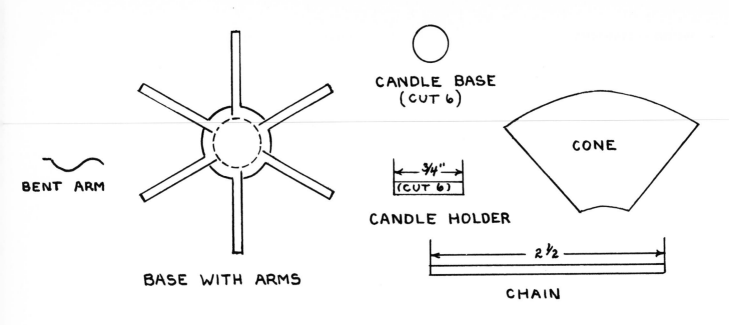

CANDLE BASE
(CUT 6)

BENT ARM

CONE

3/4"
(CUT 6)
CANDLE HOLDER

2 1/2
CHAIN

BASE WITH ARMS

CHANDELIER

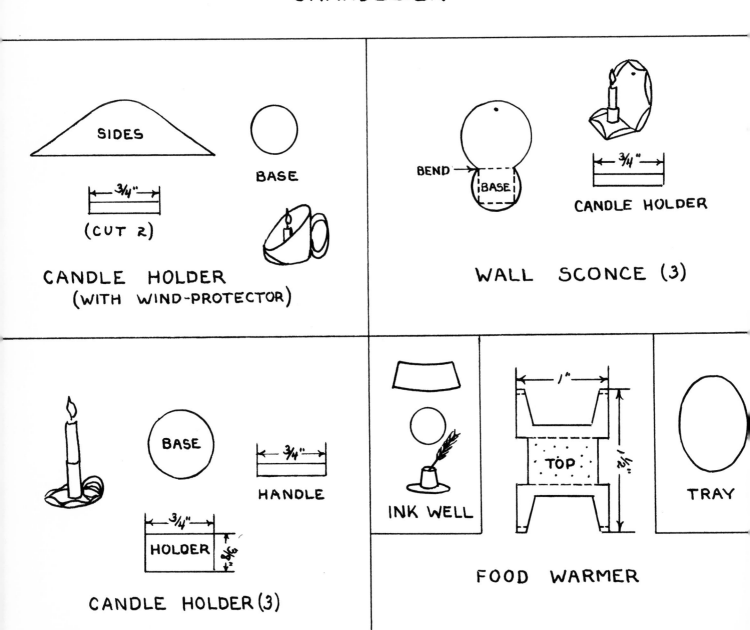

SIDES

BASE

3/4"

(CUT 2)

CANDLE HOLDER
(WITH WIND-PROTECTOR)

BEND

BASE

3/4"

CANDLE HOLDER

WALL SCONCE (3)

BASE

3/4"
HANDLE

3/4"
HOLDER

CANDLE HOLDER (3)

INK WELL

1"

TOP

1 1/2"

TRAY

FOOD WARMER

WOOD ACCESSORIES

PAINTED TRAY

1. Place tray surface flat on wax paper and glue longer sides to edges of tray, bottom flush. (Sides will extend 1/16″ above tray surface.)

2. Glue short sides between long sides and against tray edge.

3. Paint flat black and decorate as illustrated.

TOOTHPICK BROOM AND MOP

1. Cut one end off round toothpick.

2. Cut bristles for broom from an old hair brush into approximately 1 1/2″ lengths (or use unwound pieces of sisal rope).

3. Cut cotton string or yarn into 3″ lengths for mop.

4. Fasten both bristles or string with thread or fine wire around toothpick point. (Mop strings should be looped.) Glue to handle.

5. Trim bristles or string if desired.

CANDLE BOX

1. Cut the back piece as shown. Make a thumb-tack hole for hanging.

2. Glue sides to back piece, keeping bottom flush. Hold at right angles until glue sets.

3. Glue bottom against back and sides.

4. Cut front piece as shown on pattern.

5. Glue front in place against sides and bottom edge.

WALL SPICE CHEST

1. Score drawers on front piece.

2. Glue side pieces to back. Hold at right angle until glue sets.

3. Glue bottom piece to back and between sides, flush at bottom.

4. Glue edges of top of unit and place top board with 1/16″ extension in front and on sides. Back should be flush.

5. Cut top back and glue along back edge of chest and hold until glue sets.

CHIPPENDALE MANTLE CLOCK

1. Cut a clock face from a sales catalog to fit dimensions 7/8″ × 1 1/4″.

2. Cover clock face with heavy plastic, spot gluing corners.

3. Glue sides of clock face to back piece. Hold at right angles until glue sets.

4. Glue clock face to forward edge of side pieces, keeping plastic facing out.

5. Cut mitered frame for clock face.

6. Glue to plastic as illustrated on pattern.

7. Glue top board in place, flush in back.

8. Cut out top front and glue to forward edge of top board.

9. Center and glue clock unit to smaller base piece.

10. Center and glue bottom base piece to clock unit.

BEADED-EDGE MIRROR

1. Cut tin or heavy tin foil (TV dinner plate) to outside measurements of mirror.

2. Miter corners of frame.

3. Glue frame to tin with clear-drying epoxy glue.

4. Sand inside and outside edges of frame with an emery board until rounded.

5. Score the beaded edge with a pencil.

COURTING MIRROR

1. Cut a piece of tin or heavy tin foil (TV dinner plate) 1 3/8″ × 1 1/4″ for the lower section of mirror.

2. Miter corners of frame.

3. Glue frame to tin with clear-drying epoxy glue.

4. Sand inside and outside edges of frame with an emery board until rounded.

5. Glue cresting (upper portion) to top of mirror.

WOOD ACCESSORIES

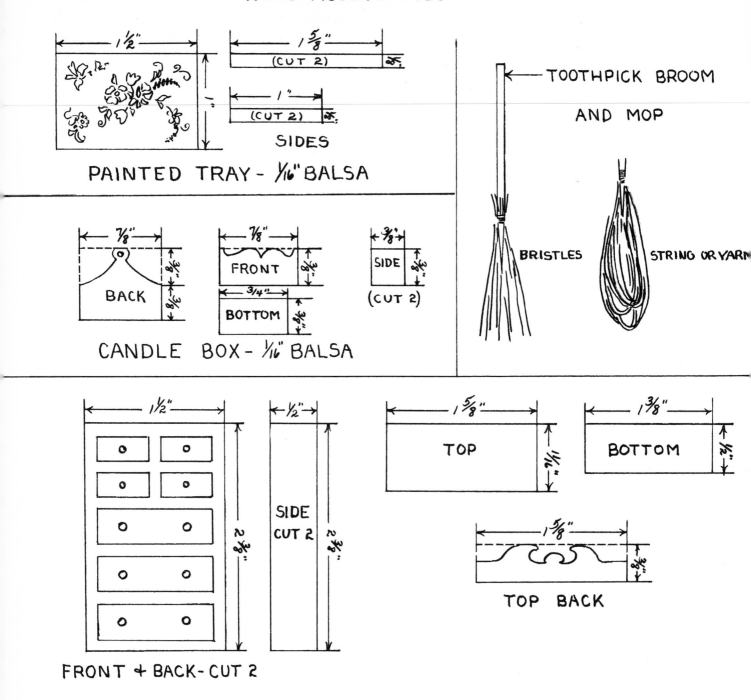

PAINTED TRAY - 1/16" BALSA

SIDES

(CUT 2) 1 5/8"

(CUT 2) 1"

1 1/2"

TOOTHPICK BROOM
AND MOP

BRISTLES   STRING OR YARN

CANDLE BOX - 1/16" BALSA

BACK   7/8"

FRONT   7/8"

SIDE   3/8"
(CUT 2)

BOTTOM   3/4"

FRONT + BACK - CUT 2

SIDE
CUT 2

TOP   1 5/8"

BOTTOM   1 3/8"

TOP BACK   1 5/8"

WALL SPICE CHEST - 1/16" BALSA

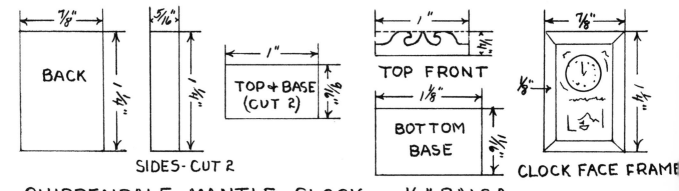

BACK   7/8"

SIDES - CUT 2   5/16"

TOP + BASE
(CUT 2)   1"

TOP FRONT   1"

BOTTOM
BASE   1 1/8"

CLOCK FACE FRAME   7/8"

CHIPPENDALE MANTLE CLOCK - 1/16" BALSA

PADDLE SCONCE
1. Glue shelf to paddle sconce.

2. See tin directions (page 108) to make candle holder for shelf.

PIER MIRROR
1. Cut tin or heavy tin foil (TV dinner plates) to the outside measurements of mirror.

2. Glue a picture (a print from a sales catalog) to upper part of frame or use tin foil for a divided looking-glass.

3. Score design on frame pieces with a dull pencil.

4. Glue frame to outer edges of mirror with clear-drying epoxy glue.

5. Glue crosspiece to divide the mirror where indicated.

STRAP SCONCE
1. Glue shelf to strap sconce where indicated on pattern.

2. See tin directions (page 108) to make candle holder for shelf.

BRATTLEBORO MIRROR
1. Cut tin or heavy tin foil (TV dinner plate) to outside measurements of mirror.

2. Miter corners of frame.

3. Glue frame to tin with clear-drying epoxy glue.

4. Sand inside and outside edges with an emery board until rounded.

PIPE BOX
1. Drill hole in back for hanging.

2. Glue sides to back with bottoms flush.

3. Score front with dull pencil to simulate drawer.

4. Glue toothpick slice to drawer center for pull.

5. Glue front to sides.

6. Glue bottom to unit.

PIPE
1. Cut toothpick stem 1 1/8" long. Sand lightly to match illustration.

2. Cut 1/8" dowel slice (1/4" long) for pipe bowl.

3. Hollow end of dowel slice.

4. Glue bowl to stem as shown on pattern.

5. A curved stem with bowl can be made from clay if desired. See Clay Accessories, page 122.

BREAD BOARD
1. Cut and glue ends to board or simulate by scoring with pencil.

FLATWARE TRAY
1. Cut hole in divider for handle.

2. Glue divider to center of tray base, allowing 1/16" at each end.

3. Glue ends to divider and base.

4. Glue sides to front and back.

BELLOWS
1. Cut two bellows shapes (including tips).

2. Sand tips slightly smaller.

3. Connect two sides of bellows by wrapping and gluing seam of tin foil (TV plate) tip. Allow a spread of 1/8" at top of bellows.

4. Glue narrow strip of fabric or thin leather between bellows sides.

MORTAR AND PESTLE
1. Shape mortar from 1/2" dowel. Hollow to dotted line as shown.

2. Shape pestle from 3/16" dowel.

ROLLING PIN
1. Shape from 3/16" dowel as illustrated on pattern sheet.

FLOWER BOWL
1. Shape from 1/2" dowel slice (1/4" long).

2. Hollow bowl to dotted line as shown on pattern sheet.

KNITTING NEEDLES
1. Shape knitting needles from ends of round toothpicks.

MUSKET
1. Carve musket from a piece of balsa 3 3/4" × 3/4" × 1/8".

2. Paint sight, trigger, and barrel flat black and stain the stock a wood color.

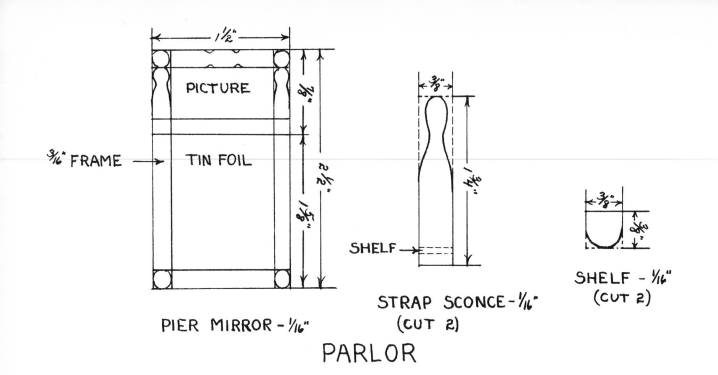

1½"

PICTURE

³⁄₁₆" FRAME → TIN FOIL

⅞"

2½"

1⅝"

PIER MIRROR - ¹⁄₁₆"

⅜"

1¼"

SHELF →

STRAP SCONCE - ¹⁄₁₆"
(CUT 2)

⅜"

⅜"

SHELF - ¹⁄₁₆"
(CUT 2)

PARLOR

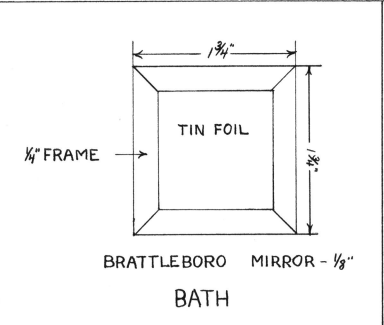

1¾"

TIN FOIL

¼" FRAME →

1¾"

BRATTLEBORO   MIRROR - ⅛"

BATH

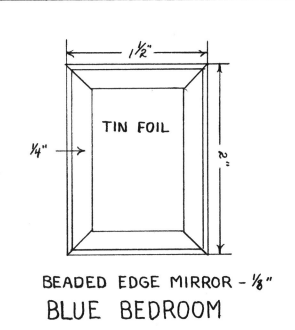

1½"

TIN FOIL

¼" →

2"

BEADED EDGE MIRROR - ⅛"

BLUE BEDROOM

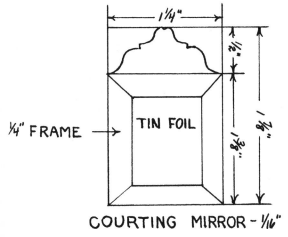

1¼"

TIN FOIL

¼" FRAME →

1½"

1⅜"

2"

COURTING MIRROR - ¹⁄₁₆"

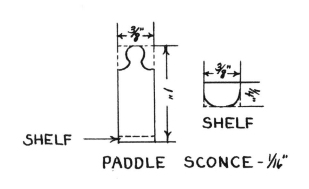

⅜"

1"

SHELF →

⅜"

¼"

SHELF

PADDLE   SCONCE - ¹⁄₁₆"

HIRED GIRL'S ROOM

From the parlor: Grandfather's chair, stool table with candle and Bible, Grandmother's chair, and braided rug.

From the blue bedroom: upholstered bedroom chair, bed steps, pencil-post canopy bed, deed box, washstand with clay accessories (from the wash area), and blanket rack.

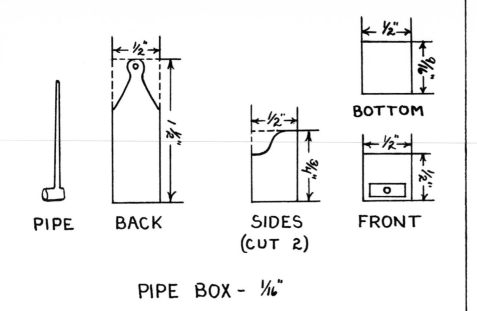

PIPE   BACK   SIDES   BOTTOM
                (CUT 2)

                         FRONT

PIPE BOX - 1/16"

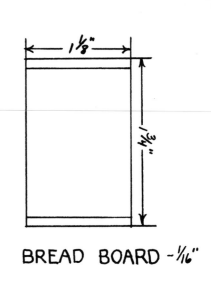

BREAD BOARD - 1/16"

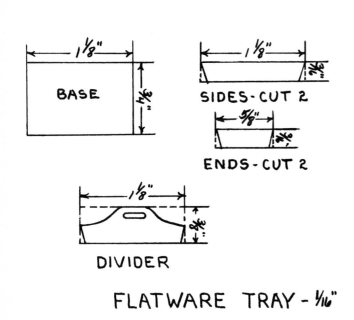

BASE   SIDES-CUT 2

        ENDS-CUT 2

DIVIDER

FLATWARE TRAY - 1/16"

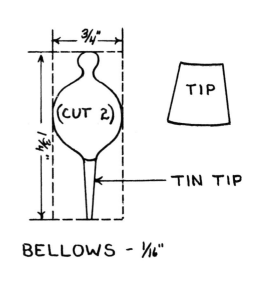

(CUT 2)   TIP

           TIN TIP

BELLOWS - 1/16"

MORTAR
AND
PESTLE

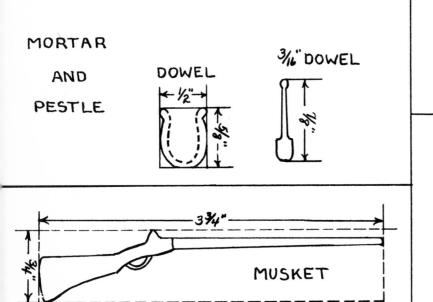

DOWEL   3/16" DOWEL

MUSKET

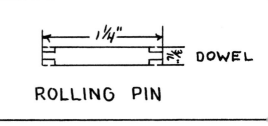

ROLLING PIN

DOWEL

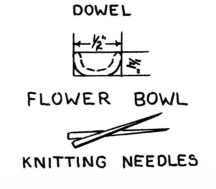

FLOWER BOWL

KNITTING NEEDLES

From the red bedroom: ball-and-bell four-poster bed on braided rug, candle stand, armoire from the wash area, and child's settle.

From the weaving room: yarn winder, six-board chest, spinning wheel, and stool.

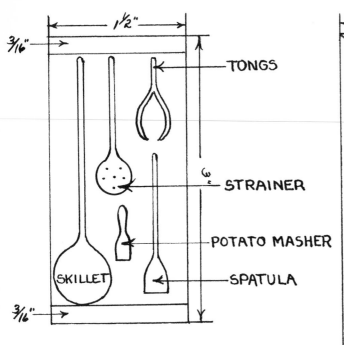

TONGS

STRAINER

POTATO MASHER

SPATULA

SKILLET

IMPLEMENT BOARD - 1/16"

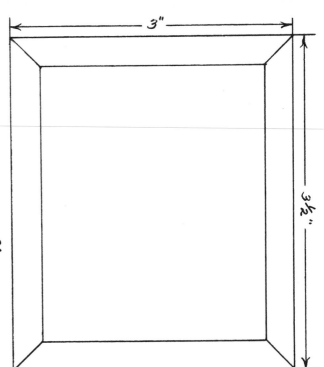

GRANDFATHER'S PORTRAIT FRAME - 1/8"
GRANDMOTHER'S - 3" x 2 1/2" x 1/8"

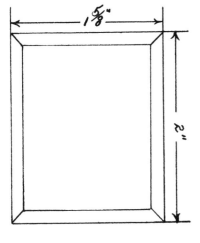

SAMPLER - 1/16"

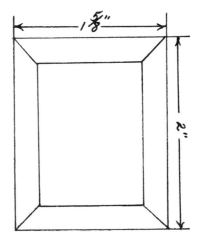

FURBER'S FRUITS (1732) - 1/8"

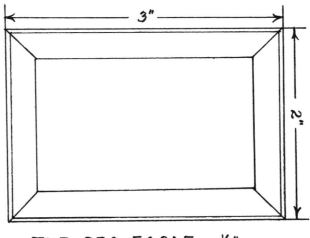

THE SEA EAGLE - 1/8"

IMPLEMENT BOARD

1. The implement board may be made with 3/16″ end-pieces or scored to simulate this construction.

2. Instructions to make the tin implements are found on pages 107–110.

3. The potato-masher is carved from a 1/4″ × 5/8″ dowel.

FRAMES

1. Frames for the pictures are made from mitered pieces of balsa wood.

2. Beading on "The Sea Eagle" is done by scoring the edge of the frame with a pencil.

3. Cut a piece of heavy plastic the size of the frame. Glue the plastic to the back of the frame. Then glue your print to the plastic (so it will be behind the "glass"). A final backing of paper may be glued to the print for protection and so that the light will not shine through. Glue only the edges, not the entire print.

4. A string, thread, or fine piece of wire may be glued to the back (one-third of the distance from the top) to hang the picture with, or it may be glued directly to the wall.

WOOD BOX

1. Glue the bottom edge of front and back pieces and place on the bottom piece. Hold in an upright position at right angles until the glue sets.

2. Glue three edges of the end pieces and set between the front and back pieces.

3. Glue string handles on each end of box or shape small pieces of wood for handles.

4. A top may be made for the box by cutting another piece the same size as the bottom piece and attaching with either lightweight fabric hinges or thin leather strap hinges. I made a second box with a lid to store wool for spinning (next to the settle in the weaving room).

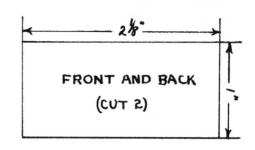

FRONT AND BACK (CUT 2)

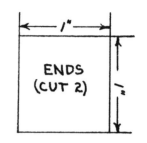

ENDS (CUT 2)

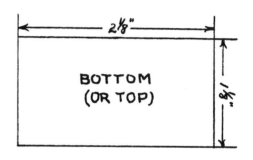

BOTTOM (OR TOP)

ADD ROPE OR WOOD HANDLES TO ENDS

WOOD BOX - 1/16″ BALSA

CARDBOARD ACCESSORIES

BUTTER CHURN

1. Bend cardboard sides into circular shape to fit bottom. (The cardboard will bend more easily if it is submerged briefly in water.)

2. Glue side seam.

3. Glue sides to bottom piece (balsa wood).

4. Measure and cut three strips of 1/8" cardboard to go around the bottom, middle, and top of churn.

5. Glue cardboard bands into place.

6. Cut 1/8" hole into top (balsa wood).

7. Insert dasher (dowel) through hole in top.

8. Stain or paint.

FIRKIN

1. Bend cardboard sides into circular shape to fit bottom.

2. Glue side seam.

3. Glue sides to bottom piece (balsa wood).

4. Measure and cut two strips of 1/8" cardboard to go around bottom and 1/8" from top of firkin.

5. Glue bands into place.

6. Cut 2 1/4" × 1/8" handle (cardboard).

7. Glue ends of handle to top band on opposite sides.

8. Glue 1/8" dowel slice to top (lid).

9. Stain or paint.

BUCKET

1. Bend cardboard sides into circular shape to fit bottom.

2. Glue side seam.

3. Glue sides to bottom piece (balsa wood).

4. Measure and cut two strips of 1/8" cardboard to go around bottom and 1/8" from top of bucket.

5. Glue bands into place.

6. Cut 2 1/8" × 1/8" handle (cardboard).

7. Glue ends of handle to top band on opposite sides.

8. Stain or paint.

From the keeping room: butter churn, two candle holders and chandelier, firkin and bucket.

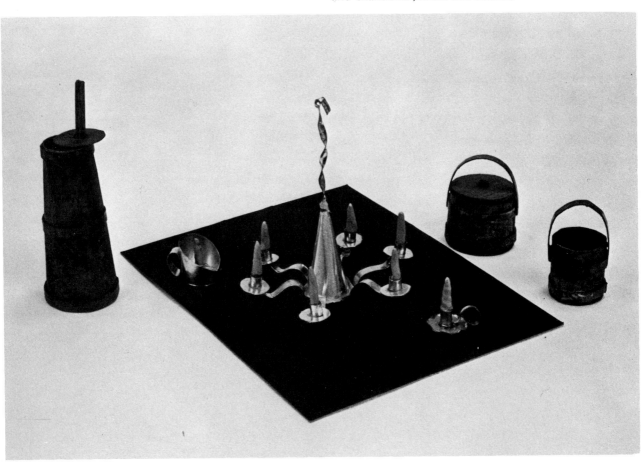

CARDBOARD ACCESSORIES
(TOPS AND BOTTOMS - 1/16" BALSA WOOD)

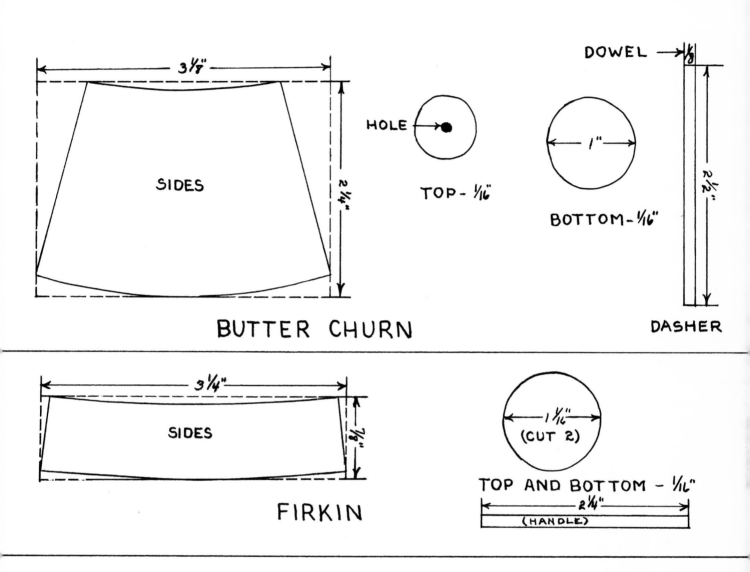

DOWEL

HOLE

SIDES

3 1/8"

2 1/4"

TOP - 1/16"

1"

BOTTOM - 1/16"

2 1/2"

1/8

DASHER

BUTTER CHURN

3 1/4"

SIDES

7/8"

1 1/16"
(CUT 2)

TOP AND BOTTOM - 1/16"

2 1/4"
(HANDLE)

FIRKIN

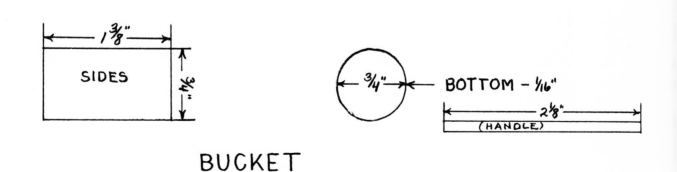

1 3/8"

SIDES

3/4"

3/4"

BOTTOM - 1/16"

2 1/8"
(HANDLE)

BUCKET

CLAY ACCESSORIES

Accessories of Sculpey or clay, and salt or bread dough (see page 106 for dough directions) must be modelled by hand with the help of small implements. As mentioned previously, I found a cuticle orange stick very useful. The smaller articles with sides, such as the ink well and cup shapes, usually start out as a ball form and are then opened by inserting an orange stick or pencil into the center, forcing the clay outward. If the article has a top, it is not always necessary to form an opening. Sculpey clay can be scooped out with a sharp instrument after baking if you want to achieve the opening. Clay can be rolled out with a rolling pin to the desired thickness and then cut and shaped for lids and flatter dishes. Handles and other long, rounded forms are simply rolled with the fingers over a smooth surface until they are the desired thickness.

Sculpey may be carved and sanded *after* baking to correct imperfections in workmanship. When adding bits of clay for handles and knobs, always try to blend in the clay smoothly to the main shape, or these parts may be baked separately and glued to the main shape. The kitty and doll are shaped from a solid piece of clay. (The doll is designed to sit in the child's settle.) A twisted effect for the andiron is achieved by simply twisting the rounded length of clay. This may be done for a twisted candle as well.

The loaf of bread is sliced after baking. A pen quill for the ink well is cut and shaped from a flat toothpick. The hand mirror has a piece of tin foil glued to the circular shape. Flowers for the vases are miniature straw flowers.

The clay accessories are painted appropriate colors with acrylic, tempera, or marker pens. A glaze may be applied with colorless fingernail polish. I painted some of the accessories, such as the andirons and some of the candle sticks, with gold paint to make them look like brass.

FABRIC ACCESSORIES

The beds all have sheets, pillows (with cases), and tufted mattresses. I used a fine white cotton for the bed linens and polyester fill for stuffing the mattresses and pillows. The mattress coverings are made out of a black and white pin-stripe cotton. The bed linens, pillows, and curtains were machine-stitched but you may prefer to stitch them by hand. (Use a small stitch setting if using a sewing machine.)

The dust ruffles for the beds are stitched to pieces of fabric the size of the mattress-rests plus the seam allowance, and go under the mattresses when the bed is made up. The dust ruffles can be glued to the bed frames but I had a housewife's compulsion to make them removable so that they could be washed eventually. The trim, however, is glued on the canopy for the pencil post bed and onto the boxed windows in the blue bedroom.

The quilt on the ball-and-bell bed is of an old design that I machine-stitched through two layers of cotton fabric with a thin layer of cotton batting between. I then scalloped the edges and hand-sewed a narrow binding around them. The coverlet for the pencil post bed is narrowly pleated by machine around the top surface of the mattress shape to give it a "boxed" look. The coverlet is fringed to match the curtains.

One problem with sewing miniature items is that a regular double-turned hem can be too bulky. It is advisable to use a single turned-up hem. You can glue the hem when using fabric, instead of sewing, but this is not as satisfactory because the glue will stiffen the fabric. Gluing the hems could be a solution to achieving pleats and folds but they must dry exactly the way they will finally hang. There is a better solution but it does take some time to accomplish. Pin the folds and pleats of the curtains and dust ruffles the way you want them to hang to a piece of corrugated cardboard. Spray the fabric several times with a "hard-to-hold" hair spray, allowing the fabric to dry between sprayings. This stiffens the fabric and keeps the folds in place.

The curtains in the red bedroom, the bath, and the chair cushions on the "great" chairs and desk bench are sewn like a pillow case (the edging for the curtains is included in the inside seam), and then turned right side out. Hem at the top for the curtain rod. The chair-cushion openings are closed by hand after being stuffed with a small amount of polyester fill. Tuft by hand. I used small fabric trim to tie-back the curtains and edge trim them. Look for suitable trimmings at your fabric store.

The curtain rods are 1/8" pine dowels hung between small screw eyes that can be purchased at hardware stores. I painted the curtain rods gold or stained them to match the molding.

The towels and blankets are tiny pieces of fringed fabric.

FLOOR COVERINGS

The braided rugs in this 1776 house are made from fine yarn (baby or sox yarn is about the right weight). Choose three colors that blend well together. Cut strands about two feet long but not exactly the same length. (When you have to tie on more yarn to make the braid longer, the knots should not come at the same place on the braid.) Tie three even ends together and secure the knot in a drawer or under a weight so that the yarn may be held taut. Braid a flat braid, moving the working area farther into the drawer as you progress, so that the braid will not twist. Tie on additional pieces of yarn as necessary until the braid is long enough to make a rug the desired size. Sew the braid (a compatible color) into circular or oblong shapes with fine thread, keeping the braid as flat as possible. Sew the end neatly together and against the last round of braid. This is called a continuous braid.

Braids may be varied as to color and pattern. Solid-color braids may be used as well as mixed-color braids. It is usually desirable to "butt" and sew the ends of a solid color braid after every round for clear definition of color. The center is a continuous braid and the end is secured before the butted rounds are added. Start with a lighter color in the center (to avoid a bulls-eye effect) and work outward alternating dark and light shades. The final round should be dark.

If you prefer a square or oblong rug with squared corners, you can achieve a very attractive and authentic colonial rug by simply sewing straight lengths of braids together side by side and allowing the loose ends to form fringe.

If your rugs do not want to lie flat, iron them with a steam iron. If that doesn't work, they may be glued with rubber cement to a piece of thin paper or fabric. Weight it with a book between wax paper until the glue dries. Trim the edges of the paper or fabric to the shape of the rug.

CLAY ACCESSORIES

JUGS   MORTAR + PESTLE   WATER PITCHER

BLUE AND WHITE POTTERY

FLAT IRON

FRUIT BOWL   SLICED BREAD   KITTY

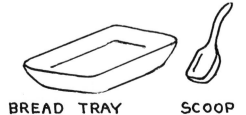  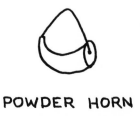

BREAD TRAY   SCOOP   DISHPAN   POWDER HORN

POTS   SPOON   ANDIRONS

BED WARMER   CANDLE HOLDERS

CHAMBER POT   INK WELL   CANES

UMBRELLA

PITCHER & BOWL   SOAP DISH   CARAFE   HAIR DISH   GLASS   SEEDS

BUTTONS   BRUSH   MIRROR

DOLL   BALL   FLOWER VASES

If the paper shows, paint the edges to match the rug. If sewing the rug seems too difficult, the braided length of yarn may be glued directly onto a base of paper or fabric into the desired shape.

For a finer braided rug, embroidery floss may be used using three strands of floss kept together. Shape and sew as above.

There are several alternatives to braided rugs. The rug in the "blue" bedroom is a piece of fringed woven fabric that was once a neck scarf. As mentioned previously, the rug in the "red" bedroom is an old needlepoint table-top doily that just happened to fit the space in the doll-house. The round fringed rug in the weaving room was also a doily.

BOOK DIRECTIONS

There are various ways to construct miniature books for your dollhouse. I used an easy method which turned out to be satisfactory but there is a more sophisticated process, more like actual bookbinding, that you may wish to try.

The simplest method, used in the Colonial Dollhouse, is to cut a piece of thin leather or cardboard for the outside cover the overall dimensions of front and back plus a bit more for the spine. Make it any size you wish, keeping in mind the scale of one inch to the foot. If you are using cardboard, you should score two "spine" lines in the center of the cardboard (wrong side) for easier bending.

Cut the pages for the book, a little smaller than the outside cover, from thin tissue paper. You will probably need five to fifteen pages, depending upon the size book you want to make. Sew along the center of the pages down the middle through all thicknesses. Use a single thread and then glue the knot and thread along the stitching line (in the back) so the thread will not come out. (See Fig. 2)

Fold the pages in half along the stitching line. Make the fold as sharp as possible. Trim the edges evenly (the inside pages will extend out farther than the outside pages). Glue the *first* and *last* pages to the wrong side of the leather or cardboard, centered along the spine and in a *closed* position. (Glue the front page and press in place, then glue the back page and *close* the cover onto it.)

Decorate the cover and spine with acrylic paint and print the title with a very small brush. I painted the edges of the Bible pages to simulate guilding (or staining) and decorated the cover with gold paint to simulate stamping.

If you want to make a more authentic book, you can cover cardboard (the thickness of cardboard that backs a pad of paper) with thin leather, velvet, or other fabric. Cut two pieces of cardboard the exact size you want the front and back covers to be. Cut a cover for the book a little larger than the cardboard plus a bit more for the spine. Glue the front and back covers to the cover material, allowing space between the cover boards for the spine, and an equal amount around all edges. Trim the corners of the cover material to the corner points of the cardboard. (See Fig. 1)

Prepare the pages as above. Trim the pages so that they will be a little smaller than the cover. You can simulate printed end papers by using a small patterned print for the outside pages. Use bookbinder's paper, wallpaper, or the inside of an envelope with the printed side facing each other when folded. (See Figs. 2 and 3)

Fold and glue the edges of the cover material to the inside over the cardboard. Glue the first and last pages of the book to the center between the cardboard. Rub with a soft cloth to get all the bubbles out.

Decorate the cover and, if you are *really* inspired, write your own book on the blank pages.

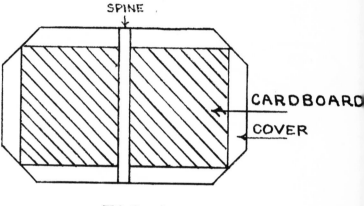

FIG. 1

FIG. 2.

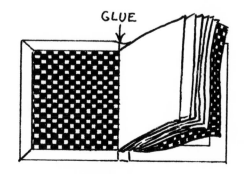

FIG. 3.

Index

(Page numbers for patterns and illustrations appear in italics.)

Accessories, 105–125; tinware, 107; wood, 11; cardboard, 120; clay, 122; fabric, 122; floor coverings, 122; (See individual item listings)
Andirons, 122, *124*
Armoire, 92, *94*

Back hall, 76; (See individual items)
Ball (child's toy), 122, *124*
Baseboards, 31 (See Trim and molding)
Bath area, 92; (See individual items)
Beams (ceiling), 7, 17, 22, *18, 19, 33*
Beds: ball-and-bell four poster, 85, *86*; hired man's, 101, *104*; pencil-post canopy, 80, *81*
Bed linens, 122
Bedrooms: blue, 77; red, 85; (See individual items)
Bed steps, 81, *81*
Bed warmer, 122, *124*
Bellow, 113, *116*
Bird's nest, 47
Blanket rack, 82, *84*
Bookcases: parlor, 74, *75*; hired girl's room, 101, *102*
Books (general), 125, *125*
Bread, 122, *123*
Bread board, 113, *116*
Bricks, 31
Broom (See Mop)
Brush, 122, *124*
Bucket, 120, *121*
Butterchurn, 120, *121*
Button dish, 122, *124*

Canes, 122, *124*
Candle, 106, 122
Candle box, 111, *112*
Candle holders: ceramic, 122, *124*; tin, 108, *110*
Candle mold, 107, *109*
Candle stands, 74, *74*; 82, *84*; 87, *87*
Carafe, 122, *124*
Chamber pot, 122, *124*
Chandelier, 108, *110*
Chairs: child's high chair, 60, *60*, Chippendale wing, 67, *68*; "Grandfather's and "Grandmother's, 70, *71*; hutch, 62, 65; ladder-back, 72, *72*; upholstered, 82, *83*
Chests: ball-feet blanket, 101, *103*; blanket 78, *79*; Penna., Dutch dower, 88, *91*; six-board, 99, *100*; spice, 111, *112*
Chimneys, 6, 31, *37*
Chippendale mantle clock, 111, *112*
Clapboards, 5
Clay (See Dough)
Clay accessories (See individual items)

Clock (See Chippendale mantle clock)
Construction: dollhouse, 7–52; furniture, 54–57
Cornices, 47, *49*
Cost, 4
Cradle (See Vermont hooded cradle)
Crane, 107, *109*
Curtain rods, 122
Curtains, 122
Cutting instructions, 55, 56

Deed box, 78, *78*
Desk-bench, 101, *102*
Desk (slant-top), 67, *69*
Dishpan, 122, *123*
Doily (See floor coverings)
Doll, 122, *124*
Doors: Christian, 7, *11*; Dutch, 47, *48, 52*; plank, 17, *20*; trap, 22, *24*; miscellaneous, 7, *10, 11, 12, 15,* 31
Dough: bread, 106; salt, 106
Drawer construction, 56
Dustcovers, 47
Dust ruffles, 122

Fabric accessories (See individual items)
Finishing (wood), 57
Fireplaces, 6, 31, *41, 42, 43, 44*
Firkins, 120, *121*
Flat iron, 122, *123*
Floor coverings, 122, 125
Floors, 7, *8, 9, 18, 19, 26, 33, 35*
Flower bowl, 113, *116*
Flower vases, 122, *124*
Flowers, 122
Food warmer, 108, *110*
Foot stool, 72, *73*
Frames, 118, *119*
Fruit bowl, 122, *123*
Funnel, 107, *109*
Furniture (See individual items)
Furniture designing, 55

Garden, 47
Glass: windows and door, 47, *50*; pictures, *118,* 119; mirrors, 113, *114*
Glaze, 122
Gluing, 56
Grass, 47
Griddle, 105, 107, *109*

Hair dish, 122, *124*
Hearths, 31
Hinging, 7, *12,* 57
Hired girl's room, 101; (See individual items)

Implement board, *118*, 119
Ink well, 122, *124*

Jugs, 122, *123*
Jointing, 54, 56

Keeping room, 58; (See individual items)
Kitty, 122, *123*
Knife, 107, *109*
Knitting needles, 113, *116*

Ladder, 22, *25*
Lighting, 47

Mat board, 6
Mattresses, 122
Metal items, 105; (See individual items)
Mirrors: beaded edge, 111, *114*; Brattleboro, 113, *114*;
    courting, 111, *114*; hand, 122, *124*; pier, 113, *114*
Mitering, 56
Molding (See Trim and molding)
Mop, 111, *112*
Mortar and Pestle: ceramic, 122, *123*; wood, 113, *116*
Musket, 113, *116*

Newel post, 31

Parlor, 66; (See individual items)
Partitions, 7, *10*, *12*, *13*, *14*, 17, *21*, 22, 31, *34*
Patterns, 54; (See also Transferring patterns)
Peg coat rack, 76
Pen quill, 113, *116*
Penna. Dutch dry sink, 62, *63*
Pipe box, 113, *116*
Pinning, 55
Pitcher and bowl (upstairs), 122, *124*
Pitcher (kitchen), 122, *123*
Plaster, 17
Pleats and folds, 122
Pottery, 122, *123*
Post and beam construction, 5, 7, *9*, *13*, 17, *18*, *23*, *33*
Pots and pans, 122, *124*
Powder horn, 122, *123*

Quilt, 122

Rockers: ladder-back, 88, *90*; slipper, 59, *59*
Rolling pin, 113, *116*
Roof: 22, *30*, 31, *32*, *33*, *38*, *39*, *48*, *49*; support structure,
    22, *27*, *28*, *29*; cap, 31, *40*; over front door, 31, *37*
Rugs (See Floor coverings)
Rush seat, 60, *61*

Sanding, 55
Sawing, 54
Scale, 6, 54, *54*
Sconces: paddle, 113, *114*; strap, 113, *114*; tin, 108, *110*
Scoring, 55
Sculpey, 7, 31, 106, 122
Seed container, 122, *124*
Settle, 98, *99*; child's, 87, *87*
Shaping a leg or post, 55
Shelves, 31, *46*
Shingles, 5, 31, *37*, *38*, *39*
Shovel, 107, *109*
Sills, 47, *48*, *51*
Sink (See Penna. Dutch dry sink)
Skillet, 107, *109*
Soapdish, 122, *124*
Spatula, 107, *109*
Spinning wheel, 96, *97*
Spoon, 122, *124*
Staining, 56
Steins, 107, *109*
Steps, 7, *16*, *17*
Stool (three legs), 99, *99*; (See Foot stool)
Strainer, 107, *109*
Supplies: dollhouse, 6; furniture, 54

Tables: half-round, 74, *75*; hutch, 62, *65*; stool, 72, *73*;
    trestle (with benches) 62, *64*
Tinware (See individual items)
Tongs, 107, *109*
Tools: dollhouse, 6; furniture, 54
Transferring patterns, 55
Trays: bread tray with scoop, 122, *123*; flatware, 113, *116*;
    oval, 108, *110*; painted, 111, *112*
Trim and molding, 6, 7, *15*, *20*, 31, 47, *48*, *49*, *51*

Umbrella, 122, *124*

Vermont hooded cradle, 88, *89*

Wallpaper, 17
Wardrobe (See Armoire)
Washstand, 92, *93*
Water bench, 60, *61*
Water dipper, 107, *109*
Weaving room, 95; (See individual items)
Windows, 5, 31, *35*, *36*, *48*, *50*, *51*
Wood: bending, 56; box, 119, *119*; selection, 54, 55
Work area, 4

Yarn winder, 97, *97*